A
stranger
in
the
family

How to cope if your child is gay

Terry Sanderson

The Other Way Press

The Other Way Press
PO Box 130,
London W5 1DQ
0181-998 1519

A Stranger in the the Family
© Terry Sanderson 1996

Second edition published 1996

British cataloguing in publication Data: a catalogue entry for this
book is available from the British Library.

ISBN 0-948982-08-X

Printed in Great Britain.

Distributed by Turnaround Distribution, 27 Horsell Road,
London N5 1XL 0171-609 7836.

For KPW as ever.

Contents

1.
Mum, Dad, I'm gay

"Mum, dad, I'm gay." These are the words that most parents hope they'll never hear from their child, and yet it's a message being delivered daily to mothers and fathers throughout the Western world.

Why this sudden explosion of young people declaring themselves homosexual? Is it that homosexuality is on the increase? Or is it simply that it's now easier for young people who consider themselves lesbian, gay or bisexual to be more honest about it?

There's little doubt that the latter is the answer. As homosexual people become increasingly reluctant to live lives of half-truth and avoidance, the drama of "coming out" is being enacted in many homes throughout the world. Individuals who in more restrictive times would have been very reticent about identifying themselves as homosexual, are now confident enough to take the step and tell the truth to those who are important to them. The AIDS crisis, too, has propelled the subject of homosexuality into the news and created a fresh awareness of gay lives and, some would say, a harsher stigmatisation of them. Unfairly, AIDS and homosexuality have become synonymous in the minds of some people. This does not take into account the fact that lesbians are — statistically — at *least* risk of infection. It is, though, a worry and burden for gay men, even though most of them will not get AIDS. I hope that a sense of proportion can be restored by looking at the facts.

If, however, AIDS is an issue for your family, then I hope this book will provide some help and comfort.

The news that your child is gay might have reached you in one of a number of ways. A survey of gay teenagers carried out by the Greater London Council (*Something to Tell You*, Lorraine

Trenchard and Hugh Warren) showed that 31 per cent of parents knew without being told that their child was gay. In about ten per cent of cases, the parents had asked, or been told by, a third party, such as a school teacher, doctor, or by other parents.

In the case of Jane and Harry, their twenty-year old son Adrian decided to tell them face to face.

"I couldn't believe it," said Jane, recounting with obvious bewilderment the moment Adrian confronted her with the truth. "He just came straight out with it: 'Mum, there's something you ought to know and I hope you won't be too angry. I'm gay.'

I couldn't take it in at first — I thought he was joking or that I'd misheard. It was as though the words weren't registering in my brain in the way that other words do; I suppose because I didn't want to hear what Adrian was saying. It was a complete bolt from the blue. I can honestly say that I'd never even suspected it. He never struck me as effeminate or different in any other way. It was only afterwards when I sat down to think about it that I started to make connections with things that had happened in the past. And when I say I thought about it, I mean I became obsessed with it: I couldn't think about anything else. I couldn't sleep for going over it in my mind. I was veering all over the place. Sometimes I was just sorry for him, then I was angry with him, then I was sorry for myself. I just didn't see how we were going to cope with it. I didn't want to talk to him, even though he tried to start conversations with me. I needed to think it through because I couldn't pin down what I really felt.

When he told his father it was a different matter; he was very angry at first and called Adrian all kinds of nasty names. He accused him of being arrogant in foisting this on us. Adrian said he was going to stay with a friend until we had decided what we wanted to do. In a way I was grateful for this because it gave Harry and me time to talk it over. In fact, Harry got himself together much faster than I did. Given he had reacted so explosively, he soon began to calm down and be more rational about it. He and Adrian had always got on so well before, and I could see it was hurting him to feel that he was apparently rejecting his son at the very time when he needed him most. On the other hand, I couldn't work out my own feelings at all. I was all confusion."

Joan, a widow in her fifties, discovered by accident the truth of her 17-year old daughter Susan's sexuality.

I was cleaning Susan's room and quite by chance I saw a letter on the floor. I normally respect Susan's privacy and I certainly wouldn't have gone searching for this letter. But I couldn't help noticing that it ended with the words 'I miss your kisses, love, Karen.' Naturally I was curious and I'm afraid I broke a promise I'd made not to read her letters or listen in to her phone calls.

It was quite obviously a love letter, and it was clear from what this other girl, Karen, said that she and Susan had been having sex. I was almost sick with the shock. When Susan came home from college, I couldn't wait and I confronted her rather aggressively with the letter. She appeared mortified that I had seen it and went red and started to tremble. But instead of being ashamed and apologetic, she admitted that she considered herself to be a lesbian and that there was nothing she could do about it. She said she truly loved Karen and that I could disapprove as much as I liked, but it wouldn't make any difference.

I often wonder whether it was really an accident that the letter was left on the bedroom floor or whether she meant me to see it. Maybe it was her way of telling me.

Diane, on the other hand, found out about her teenage son Darren from a friend of hers who felt she "ought to know". Diane is in her late forties, divorced from her husband, but living with another man, Alan. She said:

A friend of mine telephoned one evening and I could tell by the excited way she was talking that there was something she was dying to say. In the end I said: 'Come on, out with it,' and she said: 'It's about Darren. I saw him the other night in town, he was coming out of that gay club with another man. I don't know who this other chap was, but when Darren saw me he seemed so embarrassed he almost ran away. I thought you ought to know in case he's getting himself into any kind of trouble."

When she'd rung off I was trembling. I was angry and thinking: how dare she interfere in my family's business? But later I realised that I wasn't really angry with her but with Darren. There must be an explanation, I thought; he must have gone into this club with a friend for a laugh, you know how young people do. They're curious about that kind of thing, and he might just have gone to see what it was like. In the end, I thought there was no other way but to ask Darren and settle my mind one way or the other. When I confronted him he was uneasy, but not particularly enthusiastic about denying it. He said I should mind my own business and not listen to gossips, but he pointedly didn't say it wasn't true. I just kept asking and asking and in the end he admitted that he'd been in the club and that he just wanted to find out if he was gay or not.

Julian and Mary both think of themselves as reasonable people, intelligent and well-informed, and for some time they had suspected that one of their children, Rosie, was lesbian. They had no idea how they could confirm this, because although generally they had tried to be open on sexual topics, this was one which they thought would be too hurtful for Rosie, especially if their suspicions turned out to be unfounded.

We had no idea how she would react if we gently suggested that we knew about her. You know how insecure teenagers can be. If we'd been wrong, she would have hit the roof and perhaps never have forgiven us for even suggesting it," said Julian. "She'd always been a bit on the secretive side, but we wanted to help her if there was something troubling her. Finally, we decided that we would test the water and raise the subject in a general kind of way, to see what would happen. We waited until there was something about it on the television, and then Mary and I started talking sympathetically about what it must be like to be gay. All the time we were watching how Rosie was taking it. She appeared not to be listening and made no effort to join in the conversation. So Mary said to her: 'What do you think about it, Rosie?' Rosie seemed angry and said: 'I haven't got an opinion on the subject,' and walked out of the room. This just made us feel even more uneasy — it wasn't the reaction of someone who was indifferent. In the end, Mary asked Rosie outright and assured her that we weren't asking just to be nosy or to interfere or be judgmental, though when Rosie said: 'Yes, I'm a lesbian,' it still shook us. Maybe deep down we had been hoping that we were wrong.

Not all revelations came from young, single, people of course. Beryl and Adam describe the reaction they had when their 31 year old son, Benny, who was married with two children, told them he was gay.

We weren't all that surprised, but we were shocked. I'll explain what I mean. Before he got married we'd often had suspicions that Benny might be gay. I can't quite put my finger on what it was that made us think that, but it was always lurking there in the back of our minds. Perhaps it was the fact that he wasn't particularly masculine: not exactly effeminate, but then not one of your macho types. He didn't play football at school or any other boyish things. When he announced that he was getting married to a girl he'd met at work, we were thrilled to bits and put all the suspicions out of our minds. It was lovely to think that we'd be having grandchildren and an extended family. And for the first ten years everything went well. They've got on a treat, making a home together and presenting us with two lovely grandchildren. We had assumed it was all right, but apparently there was something going on under the surface that we didn't know anything about. Benny came round one day and told us that he was leaving Carol and they were both happy about the arrangement. I'll say at that point I was shocked, because I'd assumed they were so settled. It wasn't the most exciting marriage in the world, but it was better than a lot you see around. Then he told us the reason they were splitting up — he was gay and wanted to live with this other man he'd met. And that's when I say we weren't surprised, because in a way it was like the chickens coming home to roost. We were very upset that they were separating, but it seems it was all done very amicably, and a

couple of days later Carol came round and told us her side
of the story. Apparently, Benny had told her before they got
married that he had these feelings, and she'd said she was
quite happy about that. I think she imagined she could
change him once they were married. He'd not wanted at
that time to be gay, and so they'd got wed and done all the
right things. When he met this other man, he realised that
he really was gay and that was the kind of life he wanted
for himself. Carol had said she understood and they agreed
to go their separate ways, with the children staying with
her. They would consider a divorce after a year, when
Benny was sure that it was what he wanted. It was all very
civilised. It took me a long time to accept what was going
on, and I still worry about the effect it is going to have on
the children. But Benny has been living with this other man
for about nine months now, and they seem to be getting on
OK. I've got a lot of adjusting to do, and everything seems
upside down at the moment. But I'm doing my best to be
fair to everyone, and I'm supporting Benny in whatever he
thinks is right. Carol has been a tower of strength, and
seems to know all about homosexuality. Apparently they've
been mixing in gay circles for some time and she has made
a lot of gay friends.

We'll look more closely at the implications for those gay people
who marry, and at the questions of child custody and adoption in a
later chapter. But in the meantime, it is as well to realise that
social pressures have forced many gay people into marriages that,
perhaps, they now regret. The complications that this can lead to
can add further burdens on all those involved. But again, such
upheavals are survivable, and if this is an issue for you, be assured
that others have come through and found much more satisfying
ways of living for all concerned.

Don't Panic

Other young people have waited until they were away from home
before dropping the bombshell, reasoning that any bad reactions
they might get would be easier to handle if they weren't under the
same roof as their parents. Some decided that the best way to do it
was by letter, others imagined that if they suddenly appeared at

home one weekend with their new lover, their parents would somehow automatically "understand".

By which ever route the news reached you, it's likely to have created something of an emotional earthquake in your life. Now that you know, the big question is: where do you go from here?

For some parents, the first few days after the revelation can pass in a haze of shock and disbelief; for others the initial reaction is fury. Whatever your own experience, the main thing to remember at this point is that the situation is recoverable. The response that will achieve least, and which should be resisted most strongly, is panic. However angry you might be, however repulsed or bewildered, **don't take any action yet**. Impulsive decisions made while under intense emotional strain will often be regretted later. Read on.

More Than One Way

Hopefully you've realised by now that there is more than one way to react to the news that you have a gay son or lesbian daughter. I hope that eventually you will come to realise that, although your expectations of your child aren't going to be fulfilled in quite the way you imagined, the alternative might not be so bad.

Remember, too, that you are not alone. Tens of thousands of parents have passed this way before, and many more will follow. They have all had to deal with the situation according to their own conscience. There is no book of rules and no pre-formed plan to help them along. A few have given in to the immediate feelings of revulsion and dismay and have rejected their child, throwing him or her out of the family home. Others have drawn up a kind of truce which allows them to continue an uneasy relationship with their son or daughter without actually dealing with the issue. The first "solution" is not only cruel, it is also something of a cowardly method of avoiding the truth. In time, it will be deeply regretted. The second "solution" is also not really a solution at all, for it will simply prolong the agony indefinitely.

Yet other parents have made brave and determined efforts to come to terms with and really understand their child and this unfamiliar sexuality. By asking questions, parents have learned more; by facing up to their feelings they have overcome ignorance. They have taken the mystery and mythology out of homosexuality and realised that it is not, after all, something alien, but simply an alternative. Judith Brown wrote in her book *I Only Want What's Best For You*:

> We are comfortable when we feel safe, when we know what to expect of people and places. We enjoy knowing that we can cope. We want to feel that we can manage. We don't like situations that threaten us, that make us unsure. We don't like people who make us feel unsafe either. We are uncomfortable for fear they could knock us off balance. We resent them, we blame them, we close off our hearts: 'He isn't going to touch me.' We close our minds: 'There's no way I can understand him. Nor do I want to.'

I hope that you will join the brave group of those determined to progress. The rewards of enduring the pain, making the effort and facing the facts, will be a new and deeper relationship with your child.

Researchers studying families' reactions to the discovery that they have a gay child (*Homosexuality and Family Relations*, Harrington Park Press, 1990), have noted a typical pattern, expressed as a series of stages:

STAGE ONE: *Subliminal Awareness*.

There may well be suspicions within the family that one of their number is gay, although these might not be voiced. Parents and siblings might have picked up signals from the behaviour of the person they think might be gay. For instance, they may have noticed that their son or daughter has a lot of same-sex friends or shows no interest in heterosexual courtship or romance. He or she may adopt particular fashions which have 'gay' connotations (men wearing earrings or flamboyant clothes; girls dressing in a masculine fashion or wearing very short hairstyles). One woman I spoke to described how she had come to suspect that her daughter, Janice, might be gay because whenever certain topics arose, Janice invariably changed the subject or became withdrawn.

> Whenever I talked about her sister getting married, Janice would go quiet. It wasn't that she was against the wedding, it was just that the subject seemed to irritate her. I would try to get her to say what she thought about marriage and

children, but she wouldn't be drawn, she just changed the subject. It was the same whenever the family was discussing personal relationships — her brothers were quite open about their latest girlfriends and talked about them incessantly, but not Janice. She went out quite a lot in the evening, but never said anything about it when she got back. I began to wonder then whether she was keeping something from us.

When gay people get together they often talk about family events where they've been obliged to field a barrage of questions from aunts and uncles. "When are you going to get married?" they ask, or "Have you got a girlfriend yet?" They often become quite adept at dodging these questions, rivalling even politicians in their evasiveness.

STAGE TWO: *Impact.*

Impact — that's a pretty good word to describe what you're feeling at the moment. The news is out, whether by accident or design, and now you're trying to deal with it. This is the stage that this chapter is all about.

STAGE THREE: *Adjustment.*

This stage involves the initial attempts by the family to adjust to the idea of having a homosexual person as one of their number. It is at this stage that the family might put most pressure on the gay person to try to change his or her feelings, or at least to keep quiet about them. There is a fear that the family will lose status in the eyes of the rest of the community if it has someone within it who might be socially unacceptable. The what-will-the-neighbours-think syndrome is to the fore. It's also the period when most conflict might arise between brothers and sisters.

STAGE FOUR: *Resolution.*

This stage occurs when the parents — and other members of the family — discard the fantasy image they have of their child as a heterosexual and start to accept the fact that their son or daughter is gay. During this period family members begin to re-examine their own attitudes to homosexuality in the light of their daughter's or son's or sister's or brother's sexuality. It may take a long time before resolution is achieved and it may take a lot of soul-searching before it can honestly be claimed that internal conflicts have been settled.

STAGE FIVE: *Integration.*

At this stage the family will, if necessary, have changed its values in order to fully accept and integrate the homosexual family member. If there was hostility at the beginning, it will have eased and changes of opinion will have occurred, prejudices will have been modified and it will no longer be a focus of major conflict.

Reaching Integration can, for some people, be a long, drawn-out process extending over many years. There are some factors that can delay, or even halt the process of full acceptance, strongly-held religious belief is one of them. If you subscribe to a religious denomination that does not accept that homosexuality can be a valid way of life then you may have severe difficulties adjusting to the knowledge that you have a gay child. But, as we'll see later, if you are prepared to struggle with this matter, and will open your heart to other points of view, there may be another way of seeing your child's sexuality. Chapter 8 might be of help to you.

Another delaying factor might be the possession by one or both parents of strongly conforming and authoritarian personalities. People who have a very rigid respect for authority and convention often have the worst problems when they come up against something that society rejects so forcefully. To such a person, having within the family a child who is — in some people's minds — a social outcast, can be shattering.

People who place a high price on social convention or strict religious teaching will possibly 'stick' at a very early point and be unable to progress. They will have placed their child second to their desire to abide by the rules of society or the church.

Everyone has to make their own peace with their conscience, but I have a feeling that if you've come this far, you have a desire to find a way out of your distress.

Moving towards full acceptance is a process that cannot be rushed, although it can be helped along. By finding out the truth and acquainting yourself with the facts, you can more quickly come to realise that long-held prejudices aren't necessarily justified. Opinions that you had thought were cast in bronze might, in the end, have to be melted down and cast all over again. Give yourself the time you need, and resist the urge to punish yourself for occasionally having feelings of doubt about what is happening in your life. These are necessary processes for you to make a genuine leap into full acceptance.

Creative Change — Your Way Out Of The Trap.

It isn't easy, this much you know already. Since the news came you have probably experienced emotional pain such as you never knew existed. You may have shed a million tears and spent endless sleepless nights, but here's the good news: things can change for the better if you will let them! At present you might find that hard to accept and, indeed, before it can happen there have to be changes in attitudes, beliefs and, most of all, changes in the way you see your child. That is where the problems are likely to begin. Change is hard and frightening; it means facing up to the unfamiliar and taking roads that we have never travelled before. But change isn't necessarily a bad thing, it can bring long overdue improvements if we embrace it with enthusiasm.

Why do things have to change? you might ask. We were getting along nicely before all this upheaval and worry. What good has come from it all?

It might well have seemed that things were bowling along famously before you found out that your child was gay, and that since then the comfortable stability and predictability of your life has disappeared. But is it really true to say that things were getting along fine before this emotional volcano erupted?

It is clear that not everyone was happy with the situation. If your child has taken the tremendous risk of coming out to you as gay, then he or she must have found that the apparently previously happy life was, in fact, far from satisfactory. Your world may have been turned upside down, but so has your child's: he or she must have been well aware of the consequences of facing you with the truth, and probably didn't undertake it without a great deal of heart-searching. The hesitation may have extended over years, creating a form of chronic anxiety. Now that the machinery of change has been put inexorably into motion, you must decide between you what the consequence of that change is going to be.

As you consider your next move, bear in mind that if you resist changes too fiercely you will simply be conspiring to prolong your own agony. Change has a habit of happening whether we think it a good thing or not. Our choice is to accept and adjust to shifting circumstances or try fending them off. If we choose the former option we can grow and mature, if we choose the latter we can only expect to be swallowed up by forces beyond our control.

Although change is frightening it can often be good. Change allows us to grow. The writer May Sarton realised that much of our difficulty in relating to each other is caused by resistance to frequently painful change. She wrote:

> Sometimes I wonder whether what is often wrong with intimate human relations is not recognising the necessity for suffering. We fear disturbance, change, fear to bring to light and talk about what is painful. Suffering feels like failure, but it is actually the door to growth. And growth does not cease to be painful at any age.

What May Sarton had come to recognise was that human affairs are fraught with misunderstandings and unintentionally inflicted hurts. If someone is unhappy, they will naturally seek a way out of that unhappiness. If your child is trapped in the uniquely lonely world of the newly-emerging homosexual personality, then it is natural that he or she will long to escape. To do so he or she has to break down a few barriers, and that means someone will be disturbed in the process.

With One Bound He Was Free

Young homosexual people have to endure a great deal of isolation in their formative years. They will have been raised with the idea firmly planted in their mind that homosexuality is bad or funny or pathetic. When eventually they make the connection between what they have heard about homosexuality and what is happening in their own emotional life, the effect can be horrendous. Unable to tell anyone about their feelings (and the fears they induce), they absorb a constant diet of disapproval of homosexuality from their peers, their parents, their newspaper and from authority figures. The idea that they are one of these disgraceful people — who everyone seems to agree are reprehensible — can bring nothing but dismay. It is a rare child indeed who has been told by his or her parents that if their sexuality is not what everyone expects it to be, then it doesn't really matter. Most young people are told, directly or indirectly, just the opposite.

And so children who are developing with a homosexual orientation tend to retreat further and further into themselves. They find it difficult to emerge from adolescence with the strong sense of self-esteem that will be necessary to see them through life.

The famous counsellor of the parents' of gays, Rose Robertson, who founded the pioneering group Parents' Enquiry, told one interviewer that her experience had shown that young gay people often spend as long as two or three years in emotional isolation, unable to share with anyone the feelings that are troubling them.

It is during this extended period of stress that they seem to be bombarded with images of themselves that are filled with contempt. The years of confusion and isolation which young gay people have had to endure can lead to a feeling of utter helplessness. Of course, not all gay young people's experience is so bad, but they all have to endure much loneliness and doubt about their worth. It is at such times that, in other crisis situations, parents would be able to offer most support and reassurance to their children. Most parents want their sons and daughters to survive the confusions of puberty and adolescence unscathed, and try their utmost to help them through. Unfortunately this support does not often seem to extend to helping them in their discovery of an homosexual orientation. Children suspect that not only will parents not understand, but that they may be actively hostile, and so they keep quiet and simply endure the isolation.

The Crisis

Having reached the stage where the hiding, the doubt, and the guilt about lying, become too much to bear, the gay child is propelled into confiding in his or her parents. This is the signal for a major family crisis, and the initial reaction of parents to the discovery of their child's sexuality will probably include some or all of the following:

Shock: If the revelation was sudden and unexpected, the shock may be so severe it can create a range of symptoms: increased heart beats, hot flushes, shaky legs, nausea, dizziness, uncontrollable crying. One mother reported it like this:

> I don't think I've ever been so shocked in my life, it was as though someone had drained all the energy out of my body; I didn't feel as though I had enough strength even to stand up. I was trying not to show it to my son, but I think he realised and he made me a cup of tea. I was shaking like a leaf for about two hours and started sweating. It was terrible.

Anger: The news might make you furious, and often this fury is unfocused. Are you angry with your child for bringing this upheaval into your life, or are you angry with yourself for not knowing sooner? Are you angry with fate for having inflicted this particularly difficult problem on you? Or are you angry with yourself for apparently being a faulty parent and producing a defective child? Listen to Melanie, a mother of five children, the eldest of whom has recently told her he is gay:

> I was so furious with him — as though we don't have enough on our plates without this. I shouted and screamed and, I'm afraid, called him some pretty choice names. He was so upset because he'd come to me for sympathy and here I was going on like he'd just committed mass murder. But I really was angry, and I found it very difficult to control myself. I suppose it's my temper. I just couldn't stop myself because he'd roused up all these doubts about what I'd done wrong and how we were going to tell the rest of the family and whether it was because his dad was working away from home. I really could live without all that at the moment.

Such doubts and confusion are common and, in the circumstances, understandable, but you should try not to let them push you into hasty action which you might later regret. Accept the anger and let it take its course, but resist the urge to act on it for the time being. Anger does not always provide the best basis for clear-headed, creative decisions.

Disbelief: Your child has told you something that you didn't want to hear and naturally in your shocked and vulnerable state you will be looking for a way out. As a defence mechanism disbelief is very useful. "He's just doing this to upset us, it isn't really true," is the immediate reaction of some parents or "She doesn't understand what she's saying, it's just a mistake on her part" or "It's a phase that will pass. All children go through this." This was Marie's reaction to her son's coming out:

> He was only seventeen and I didn't see how he could possibly know at that age that he was a homosexual. I said to him: 'All boys go through a phase like this, you'll get over it.' But he was adamant that he knew his own mind. He said he'd tried to go out with girls and it just wasn't right for him. I told him not to be so stupid, that he couldn't know and that things would work out. I told him I didn't want to hear any more about it, he was just being silly.

This, for some parents, is the end of the whole business. They decide it isn't true, and refuse to hear any more on the topic. The reasoning goes: if I don't know about it, then it doesn't exist. The child's honesty has been rebuffed because the parents don't want to deal with the implications. But like it or not, once the news is out it can't be put back again. Even though you purport not to believe your child, somewhere in the back of your mind a persistent little voice will not let you forget that you have a problem you haven't dealt with. If you refuse to believe what your child has said, the problem has nowhere to go and must remain festering and unresolved, poisoning your relationship with your son or daughter indefinitely. You may not lose him or her immediately, but you can be sure that in the long term a groaning abyss will open between you.

Revulsion: Many people and that includes otherwise ordinary, loving parents feel a very strong antipathy towards homosexuals. It isn't uncommon to hear normally compassionate men and women saying: "The very idea of what they do makes me feel sick" — and meaning it quite literally. These overwhelming feelings of revulsion are not affectation; they are a symptom of homophobia. We will examine this phenomenon in more detail in a later chapter, but at the moment, those people who feel this way about homosexuals and homosexuality should, for the sake of their relationship with their child, try to contain their disgust. An unbridled display of abhorrence at this stage might have a deeply damaging effect upon you and your child. While the prospect of having a homosexual in the family might make you feel physically ill, try, for everyone's sake, to keep it under wraps for the time being. Here is Derek, telling of his reaction to his son Mark's announcement that he was gay:

> I was sick to tell you the truth, I mean physically sick. I find everything about homosexuality absolutely revolting and obscene. Thinking about what two men do together gives me the shudders, and I told him so. I said: 'If that's what turns you on, you're as disgusting as they are. No son of mind would feel that way.'

Fear: One of the most fearful words that spring to mind when a someone we love comes out as gay is AIDS. The first thing parents want to know from their newly come out son is: "Have you got AIDS" The hysteria generated by AIDS naturally worries parents, and its presentation in the early days as "the gay plague" leads many to assume that it is a problem confined entirely to homosexual men. In truth, however, AIDS is still a relatively rare condition in Britain, even among gay men (in other countries, particularly in the developing world and in some big cities in the USA, this is sadly not the case). Of course, it is possible that your son has come into contact with the Human Immunodeficiency Virus (or HIV, as the virus that can lead to AIDS is called), but you shouldn't immediately assume that this is the case. The odds are stacked in his favour that he is completely unaffected.

Although AIDS is a medical condition, it has taken on an almost supernatural significance in the minds of many people. The sensational press coverage of the Syndrome has not helped. Later in this book we will take a more studied look at what AIDS means for gay people and their families, as well as for the rest of the population, who are not, despite the emphasis on homosexuality, immune to HIV infection. In the meantime, don't assume the worst.

Self-blame

When a child seems in any way imperfect, a common parental reaction is to look inward and ask: "Where did we go wrong?" Whether the problems are emotional, physical or a matter of sexuality, there can be a tendency for parents to blame themselves for what they see as their "flawed creation". But the idea of perfect children, or ideal parents, is an illusion, and a very damaging one at that. Parents who torment themselves with this fantasy should try hard to let go of the idea that anybody can be faultless. It is a burden that is totally unnecessary and unrealistic. If we refuse to accept each other, warts and all, we are asking for constant disappointment and disillusion. Like it or not, our innate human frailties will inevitably become apparent. We must let go of the idealised image of family life which is projected by films, books and advertising — it rarely exists in the real world.

Sorrow

Sadness overwhelms many parents when they discover the truth about their child's sexuality. They feel sorry for their son or daughter because they imagine that life has dealt them a losing hand. "My child is doomed to the life of an outcast: lonely, rejected, different." Stated as baldly as that, there seems to be every reason for sorrow, but as we look more carefully at the subject we'll see this reaction is premature. The popular image of the homosexual as the perpetual outsider, denizen of some sordid underworld, is very rarely a true one. Those with acceptance and support from their families have enough self-esteem to avoid the traps.

This is how Gail felt about her daughter Lisa:

I was so sorry I cried for three nights solid after she told me. I couldn't help thinking about what she was going to miss in life. She wouldn't have children, she wouldn't be able to bring her partner to all the family gatherings, she wouldn't be accepted by so many people. I imagined that she would be very lonely. She'd grow old all alone and end up some crusty old spinster who everybody laughed at. It made be extremely sad.

Looking For A Cure

After the news has been broken, some parents fly into a panic, looking for instant answers to something which they don't want to accept. For such parents the first response is: How can we cure it? Phil and Judy had such a reaction:

> When Helen told us about herself my first thought was: DOCTOR", says Judy. "After all, at that stage I imagined homosexuality was some kind of illness, a mental illness that could be cured. If we could find her the right psychiatrist, perhaps she could be persuaded out of it. I wanted to make an appointment with our GP, so he could tell us the best course of action, but Helen wouldn't have any of it. She said she wasn't ill, and that she didn't need treatment, but I was running round like a headless chicken trying to find a way out. I was looking for answers everywhere and anywhere — except in the right places. I even went to a fortune teller, and she said it was a childish phase that Helen would grow out of. I didn't like to tell her that Helen was twenty-seven.

Rejection

In a small number of cases, parents find they are unable to contain or control their initial anger and revulsion. Their first impulse is to push their child away and, in the process, relieve themselves of the pain that they are enduring. They would rather their child was physically apart from them than try to see what can be done to help the situation. Their fear and loathing of homosexuality can be so strong that it even overcomes their parental instincts to protect. In such cases children are occasionally expelled from the family home, cast aside and told never to return. Sometimes this is just a temporary state of affairs, but in a few cases the parents cannot overcome their revulsion, with the result that they lose their child completely.

In an interview with Dee Remington in the magazine *Family Circle*, a mother, Gill Summers (not her real name), related her experiences when her son Chris came out to her as gay. She says that it tore her family apart, particularly as her husband, Mike, could not come to terms with it in any way. "There was nothing else I could do," she says, "I agonised over it for weeks, but I knew I had to tell Chris to go." The family could not accommodate Chris's sexuality, they became fixed in a mind-set that was self-fulfilling and circular: 'I can't tolerate homosexuals, Chris is a homosexual so I can't tolerate Chris'. Gill Summers says that the family felt "stabbed in the back" by Chris's decision to tell them he was gay. Since he left home and went to live with an older man, Gill has only a remote relationship with her son, and doesn't know how to improve it.

That sad and destructive circle can be broken. If you feel that the only way to cope is to push your child as far away from you as possible, please wait. Don't cast him or her out of your life. Don't deprive them of the home and love that is needed at this critical moment. It may be that even after you have had time to consider the alternatives you still feel that physical apartness and disowning is the best answer. But at least wait a little while to be sure. Once the family is smashed apart, it is almost impossible, as Gill Summers found, to put it together again.

The Bereavement Effect

These initial reactions, although violent and intense, are often short-lived. They can be damaging, but the situation is still recoverable. Once the initial shock begins to wear off, parents may begin to ask questions of themselves and their children which are no less distressing than the first few weeks of sheer misery. It begins to dawn on mum and dad just what the implications of their child's announcement are.

Gradually they come to regard their beloved son or daughter as not the person they had imagined them to be. Suddenly there is a stranger in the house, someone who you thought you knew but who, in fact, has turned out to be somebody else — somebody you'd rather wasn't a member of the family.

One mother, Dilys, said:

> I began to look at my daughter Carole quite differently after she told me she was lesbian. I had always thought of her as an ordinary, conventional girl who would do ordinary conventional things. She had never shown any big ambitions to be a career-woman or anything like that, and no indication that she had any special talents. I had just

assumed that one day she would settle down with a man and have children, like everyone else. She had always had a sensible head on her shoulders and didn't act silly when she was younger. Then all of a sudden, when she was twenty-four, she comes to me and tells me she's moving out. When I asked where to, she calmly says she's moving in with another woman called Anna. There was never any doubt from the beginning what was going on, she didn't make any secret about it, like pretending she was just a flatmate or anything.

It took me a long time to come to terms with it. I spent hours and hours trying to work it out. I mean, Carole hadn't shown any special interest in other women, although thinking about it, she didn't show any interest in men, either. She hadn't been a great one for boyfriends, but I'd assumed that was because she was a bit shy.

We were always very close, though. We were more like friends than mother and daughter, and we were even closer when her father died. She was a great support through that time. But then she dropped this bombshell and suddenly I couldn't bring myself to look at her. I felt strange in her company. She was carrying on as usual, as though nothing had happened, but the Carole that I'd known for the previous twenty-four years was suddenly replaced by this woman who was saying she was a lesbian.

To my knowledge I've never met a lesbian before, but I've often heard about them. In a factory where I used to work, we'd make jokes about the other girls, but it was never serious. I just couldn't accept it, and I felt that I'd lost Carole for good. Even though she came round to see me every day after she moved in with this other woman, I still didn't feel it was the same girl. I got very depressed, very much like I did when my husband died. You know what I mean? It was like I'd been so used to having him around and then all of a sudden he wasn't here any more, and I was looking for him. It was a bit like that with Carole, I was missing the old Carole that I knew and trusted, and I couldn't get used to this new version who was living with another woman, and doing God knows what with her.

Counsellors who work with the parents' of gays recognise this phenomenon and call it the Bereavement Effect. It has many symptoms in common with those experienced when someone in the family dies. The previously beloved son or daughter suddenly seems to disappear from life and is replaced by a sinister version of the same person. Parents begin to grieve for what they have lost. Their expectations, which have been taken for granted for so long suddenly need to be reassessed and, in some cases, completely abandoned. It's unlikely, for instance, that there will be grandchildren from that source; there will be no wedding and, at least in the formal sense, no in-laws or extended family. This can be particularly distressing for the parents of an only child. For them the majority of their hopes for the future may have been invested in their son or daughter, and when that hoped-for future disappears, they may be devastated.

It's not an easy thing to accept, but I hope you will see that there are positive alternatives which your gay child can bring into your lives. Don't give up on the future just yet.

As with other forms of bereavement, the sense of loss will eventually give way to acceptance, and then a form of adjustment to the new situation. For most people that means a calmer, less fevered approach. It isn't so much that they're happy with what has happened or that they've made any progress at all in sorting out their feelings, it's just that distress on this scale cannot be tolerated for long periods. It's too exhausting! The mind will not allow itself to be stressed indefinitely in this manner, and will soon find a way to cope. The intense agitation felt at the beginning will gradually wane.

We've already looked at some of these avoidance mechanisms: refusing to believe the news and rejecting it out of hand; believing it but pushing it to the back of the mind; accepting it but disapproving and, most drastic of all, getting rid of the problem by throwing the child out. The use of such techniques ensures that you won't make much progress in bringing you and your child back together.

A much better approach is to ask questions, seek out people who know the answers, read extensively on the subject, talk endlessly to your son or daughter about what it is like to be a gay person. Rather than setting your mind in concrete with phrases like: "It's wrong and nothing can make it right" or "I don't understand it and I never will", start to say to yourself: "I may not like it, but at least I can give it a hearing."

During this second phase, any combination of the following effects may be experienced:

Dismissal

This is an extension of the disbelief that greeted the first discovery of your child's sexuality. Not only do you refuse to believe what you've been told, you now dismiss the matter totally, refusing to listen to what your child is telling you and rejecting out of hand any evidence which might be produced. "It's just a phase...", you said at first. Now that has been extended to "...and I don't want to hear any more about it."

If your son or daughter persists in raising the issue, you immediately change the subject. You reject any mention of homosexuality, and if you do happen to see references to it on television or in the newspaper, you quickly pass it by with a feeling of annoyance.

But even with your best efforts to dismiss the topic from your thoughts, your subconscious mind is more pragmatic and refuses to let go of the knowledge quite so easily. Your sleep may be disturbed, you may feel curiously tired and depressed. Although you won't admit it, this "non-existent" problem is really getting you down.

Withdrawal

Some parents will accept the news, and might even say that they don't mind. But then their attitudes to their child, and maybe other members of the family, change. The parent withdraws from those who are important, especially the gay child. It's a means of avoiding the truth, of course. If you can distance yourself emotionally from your child, you don't have to face truths about him or her that you find unpalatable.

This creates a dismal and downbeat atmosphere at home. Everyone knows there's something going on, but no-one seems to know what to do about it. The whole family is affected.

Blaming

Having assimilated the news, but not come to terms with it, some parents begin looking for a scapegoat. They may turn on their gay child and put the blame for their unease on his or her shoulders. "Why have you done this to us?" they might say. "It's so selfish of you."

This is the parents' way of dealing with something they don't know how to handle in any other way. It is something totally outside their experience and understanding, and they simply grasp the first way out. Blaming the messenger for the bad news is an age-old human reaction: the fundamental injustice of it isn't hard to see.

Balancing

Sometimes mothers and fathers find that the whole household has been sent into turmoil by the revelation. Brothers and sisters, grandparents, aunts and uncles — a whole disparate group of people are trying to cope in their different ways. And sometimes parents feel it is their duty to try and keep the peace during this volatile time. A balancing act has to be achieved; aggressive reactions and disapproval have to be weighed against defensiveness and confusion. Whilst this is going on, parents' own feelings are being neglected and suppressed.

Choices

Now perhaps a couple of weeks have passed, or even a couple of years. Parents have still not been able to deal with their son's or daughter's revelation because nobody prepared them for it. No parenting book, no advice from their own parents and no previous experience can help them: they have to make their own rules for this particular family crisis.

Somehow they have managed to live with it and make an uneasy peace with the news, but still they worry. They don't know exactly what to expect in the future. Maybe still they are harbouring feelings of anger or revulsion which they keep suppressed because they have no more energy to express it.

There may be a kind of truce with their child, in which both parties have an unspoken agreement that they won't talk about the issue. After all, enough pain is enough. "All right," some parents might say, "You've told us, we know. Now let's forget it and get on with our lives as before."

That might relieve the immediate, acute pain but it does nothing to deal with the bigger pain that will, if you don't tackle it, haunt you for the rest of your life.

It is now that you have a series of choices to make: either to work on improving and resolving the problems, or ignore them and hope that they will somehow disappear. If you opt for the second choice, then there is nowhere to go. You will simply drift, out of control, never being able to have a proper relationship with your son or daughter again. Any important emotional development that takes place in his or her life will not be shared with you. Instead of being a source of joy, your child will be a source of apprehension and fear. He or she, in turn, will not feel comfortable telling you about events that are important to his or her future happiness. What makes him happy will, by inference, make you miserable.

Opting for the first choice — to boldly face the cause of your unhappiness and work to change it — is a hard one, but in the end it will bring rewards greater than you ever imagined. Deciding that changes are necessary is never easy, but then, nothing worth having is!

Squaring up to what is really going on in your child's life means that not only will you stand every chance of creating a new and more rewarding relationship with him or her, but you will also gain new insights into the whole of your family. In the process, it is likely that you'll become a bigger, better, more loving human being. This could well provide you with a new way of looking at the world.

You may not like the idea of shaking up your particular jumble of prejudices and attitudes at the moment, but when you start you'll find it can become pleasantly addictive. Once you begin challenging one set of assumptions, you begin to realise that there are a whole lot more that could do with a dusting down. You will learn not only how to love your children in a different and better way, you will also learn how to let them go. And the wonderful contradiction is that by letting them go, you stand a better chance of staying close to them.

There is other positive news. After years of doubt and hesitation, your child has been honest with you about something of great importance in their life. And although all may seem chaos at present, it is a sign that he or she has emerged from the depths of despondency as a stronger person — strong enough and sure enough to be able to share with you the inner knowledge that such a long process of self-examination has brought. As Ken Plummer, a lecturer in sociology, has written:

> Coming out to the straight world is often the first sign that the homosexual person has successfully navigated his own problems and has moved on to those of others.

Your son or daughter is now inviting you to navigate your own problems in the hope that you will emerge at the other end as strong and determined as they are.

Emergency Action

You've just come through the trauma that's been termed coming out, and naturally you're looking for ways to cope. How do you get through these first few days and weeks until you can work out your own approach?

The most common complaint I have heard from parents on hearing the news of their child's unconventional sexuality is that it has become something of an obsession. They say that they "can't stop thinking about it" or "can't get it out of their mind". Many say that sleep is disturbed: as soon as their head hits the pillow, the waking nightmare begins. All the doubts and uncertainties that have been plaguing them during the day seem to take on a new and disturbing intensity at night. Three o'clock in the morning is a lonely time for anyone, and for those with a worrying preoccupation, it can be doubly trying.

During the day, the normal routine becomes just another focus for the worries. You can't think properly about much else; work suffers, relationships with other people become clouded. Even if you manage to forget about it for a few minutes, there is a sudden jolt when it hits you again.

The anxiety becomes a constant companion, a wearying fact of life. There is no rest from the realisation that you have a son or daughter who is different, and who might be facing a life of isolation and rejection. To combat such a level of anxiety, the mastery of a relaxation technique can be invaluable.

There are a number of useful books which will help you master relaxation, and audio and video tapes are also available. Take a look in your local bookstore and music shop for an idea of what's on offer. Or alternatively find a counsellor or relaxation group in your area.

Talk to a trained or specialist counsellor

If you are finding it difficult to manage on your own and need to talk things over with someone, please be careful who you choose. Well-meaning friends and relatives might turn out to be the worst people for the job. Often they will be ill-informed, confused and just as upset as you are, and will simply reinforce your fears. If you are desperate to voice your worries, then you might find a trained counsellor would be the best person to turn to. Not only would he or she be impartial, but you would get a much more constructive approach to your problem.

Your local library may have a list of qualified counsellors in your area, or you could ring the local branch of Relate (formerly The Marriage Guidance Council) which will have a team of highly-trained staff, sympathetic to your situation. Relate does not deal only with marital problems, but with anything which is troubling individuals or couples.

Don't forget, too, that other parents have set up support groups just for people in your situation. You'll find a list of them in the back of this book. Even if you don't find one in your area, you could still ring a distant one and have a chat. The cost of the long distance call will be money well invested.

2.
Why can't I accept?

There is widespread ignorance about homosexuality and how it fits into people's lives — an ignorance shared by many parents. Most of us are raised either to despise homosexuality or to imagine that it has nothing whatever to do with us. And even if we have come across homosexuality before — in a work colleague perhaps — we are unlikely to have imagined that it would ever have anything to do with our own family.

This lack of knowledge, and desire not to think about the subject, has led to a number of pre-formed stereotyped ideas about homosexual men and women. For instance, gay men are often presented as limp-wristed, weak and effeminate, while lesbians are portrayed as masculine in appearance and aggressive by nature. Alternatively, gay men are seen as sinister figures, obsessed with sex and inhabiting dubious night-clubs, while lesbians are seen as seething man-haters. The mass media repeatedly reinforce these images of homosexuals as either sad, sinister, hilarious or unimportant. In many ways, gay people themselves collude in the process by remaining quiet and hidden, preferring not to contradict the negative images. Many gay people stay silent about their sexual orientation because they fear that if the truth were known, they would fall victim to the discrimination which they see all around them. They are careful not to contradict the false assumption that they are heterosexual so as not to put at risk their jobs, accommodation or the regard of the significant people in their lives.

Naturally, if you have been raised to imagine that gay men and lesbians are either monstrous or pathetic, and you have had this view confirmed on an almost daily basis by newspapers, then it will be somewhat dismaying to find that one of your deeply loved children has turned out to be gay. Aren't homosexuals those dreadful people that *The Sun* and *The Daily Star* are constantly "exposing"? Aren't they the people who eat up all the rates, and demand special privileges and break up families and abuse children? Aren't they the individuals who are always appearing in the agony columns as lonely, desperate people who cannot make anything like a real relationship? And isn't it homosexuals who flaunt themselves on television, demanding 'rights' and being a general nuisance, or dressed up in silly costumes and make-up, mincing about in situation comedies?

You can see from this small list how pervasive and prevalent the negative attitudes are. Nowadays there is a bit of balance, and sympathetic gay characters have appeared in most popular soap operas. Even then, such portrayals still bring forth outcries from those who would prefer that the subject were not raised at all in public.

Despite attempts to improve the image of gay people via TV drama, I've often heard cynical heterosexuals — mainly right-wing columnists in reactionary newspapers — saying that "there's no smoke without fire" and that homosexuals deserve their unsavoury reputation. We are told that "everyone knows" that homosexuals can't be trusted or that they are promiscuous or are incapable of making their relationships last. It's very difficult to come to anything but a sad conclusion when popular newspapers dwell constantly on the negative aspects of gay life while denying that gay people can have good qualities, too. You'd be hard-pressed to find stories in Britain's tabloid press that tell of noble acts by gay people or of their valuable contributions to society. Even though there are many admirable homosexuals, they aren't acknowledged as such. It wouldn't fit the traditional picture.

Homophobia: the name of the beast

There is no doubt that the fear and hatred of homosexuals is common in our society and, in his book *Society and the Healthy Homosexual*, Dr George Weinberg gave this special antipathy a name: homophobia. Labelling it a "phobia" is, in many ways, apt. Many people who are deeply hostile towards lesbians and gay men experience feelings which mirror the symptoms of other severe phobic reactions: increased heart rate, trembling, nausea, anxiety and an inexplicable fury. They may sometimes feel violently aggressive, and this can manifest itself in what has come to be known as gay-bashing.

There are lesser degrees of the condition, when the homophobic individual becomes mildly agitated or maybe only slightly uncomfortable in the presence of (or at the thought of) homosexual people. In such cases there is no loss of control and the hostility might show itself in more subtle ways such as unspoken but obvious disapproval, avoidance, rejection, criticism and a desire to humiliate the object of their loathing. Homophobia can show itself in thoughtless acts that make life very difficult for the gay people who have to endure them. Here is the experience of one gay man who, when he came out at work, found himself on the receiving end of a colleague's homophobia:

> There was this one woman in the office who started being very bitchy to me, she just wouldn't let the subject drop. Day after day I had to put up with her snide remarks, about how she wouldn't like her son to meet me and how none of the men in the building were safe. I could put up with that, although it wasn't very pleasant. Then she began to say that I might have AIDS, and other people started talking about it. She had everyone worried, and eventually I had to go and see the boss. He said that I'd better keep my private life out of the office, and if this kept on I'd have to look elsewhere for a job. He said he didn't like his staff being in turmoil as it affected their work. I felt very hard done by — I was being blamed for this woman's nasty mindedness.

Homophobia is an insidious beast, splitting families and friends apart, causing otherwise rational people to persecute their fellow citizens, and even turning gay people against themselves. This latter phenomenon, when homosexuals themselves become anti-gay, is known in the gay community as "internalised homophobia" or sometimes "self-oppression".

Anti-homosexual prejudice is so deeply ingrained in our culture that there is little wonder so many gay men and women feel badly about their sexuality; self-hatred causes much misery for them. It is likely that your child has felt badly about him or herself for a long time, and only recently has begun to see that there are alternative ways of looking at their orientation. Like you, your son or daughter may be having a great deal of trouble shaking off the doubts and fears about homosexuality, and may be badly in need of reassurance.

Occasionally, though, the people who are most averse to homosexuals, and who speak out most fiercely against them, are the ones who must face the problem within their own families. A case in point was the former Chief Constable of a large English city, who hit the headlines in 1986 after making a strongly-worded speech condemning homosexuals. His words were harsh and unforgiving; he judged gay people to be morally reprehensible and "swirling around in a cesspit of their own making." His religiously-inspired speech was widely reported and led to an enormous expression of hatred for gay people throughout the country. However, shortly afterwards a Sunday newspaper revealed that the Chief Constable's own daughter was lesbian. It wasn't clear whether he had known this when he made his speech, and we can only guess how he coped with the aftermath of discovering that one of the "monsters" he had condemned was actually his own child.

We all have prejudices — some of them justified, some of them irrational — most of the time we learn to live with them. They are small matters that don't trouble us much in our day-to-day life. Sometimes, however, our fixed and preconceived ideas are based on ignorance and misunderstanding, and can stand in the way of our efforts to find happiness and fulfilment; they become a nuisance and a real obstacle to our functioning. When that happens, we must consider what action we can take to rid ourselves of these troubling feelings.

Although there are some similarities between phobias and prejudices, there is no doubt that prejudices are far more difficult to tackle. Prejudices are not under the control of our logical mind, they are part of our emotional construction. Reason alone won't make many inroads into prejudice. If, you have a deeply-held prejudice against homosexuals, then discovering you have a gay child won't necessarily change it. However, the discovery of your child's secret will have set up a conflict in your mind. On the one hand you have someone whom you love and cherish, someone in whom you have invested a lot of time, effort and pride; on the other hand you have found that this person is homosexual. How are you going to reconcile the two incompatible facts which now cannot be separated? Consciously or unconsciously, one side of your head might be telling you "I can't stand homosexuals" while the other will be shouting "But I love my child who is a homosexual."

Researchers have discovered that it's almost impossible to educate or reason prejudices out of existence. For instance, you can teach a racist that if his hateful opinions were to be carried through to their logical conclusion, they would result in an almost endless catalogue of misery and bloodshed in the world. You can teach him until the cows come home that judging people on the colour of their skin is preposterous, but he won't believe you. Even if you produce ten volumes of evidence from history and experience to back up your contention, his racism will remain. You can argue that his opinions are inhumane, unfair and unjust but, however eloquent you are, it will have no effect; his prejudice will stay intact. He is convinced that people who belong to different cultures deserve unfair discrimination. The only way you could change his opinions would be to dent his prejudice with some kind of personal experience on an emotional rather than an intellectual level. This experience would have to be intense enough to cause him to reassess the way he felt about people from different races.

The same principles apply to prejudiced reactions to homosexuals. It will take an emotional experience to challenge any long-held homophobia you might harbour. And this is where you're off to a flying start: that all-important personal, emotional experience has come to you by courtesy of your gay son or daughter.

However, the analogy between racial prejudice and homophobia is not precise. In our society it is no longer generally acceptable to express overtly racist opinions and it is against the law to discriminate on grounds of race or ethnic origin. Society shows no such restraint in relation to homosexuals: it is quite acceptable in most circles to make crude jokes, slanderous remarks and hurtful comments about lesbians and gay men, even when they are present. There is no law which protects homosexuals from discrimination.

There may be a protracted internal battle between your uncomfortable feelings about homosexuality, and your need to continue loving your child. At this very moment, though, your subconscious mind is working on the matter. Even though you may feel, on the surface, like a mass of confusion, your inner mind is beavering away, making comparisons, weighing the gains against the losses, and will eventually tell you which is most important: your prejudice or the quality of the relationship you have with your child. The revelation may be gradual and subtle, but you can be sure that it will happen.

This chapter is about helping you along the way by presenting some facts about homosexual people and their place in the world. It will attempt to challenge some of the myths, answer some of the questions which parents most frequently ask, and back it all up with the latest research findings.

Knowing the facts won't necessarily make you immediately easier about the whole subject, but being better informed can help you sort out what is really important. By enlightening yourself about the nature of homosexuality, your mind will have the relevant data to help it along. So let's examine some of the common misapprehensions about homosexuals.

What follows is a list of some of the things that you may have believed, or half-believed, simply because you had no reason not to. When the subject seems exotic and irrelevant there is little need to peer very closely at it. But when it threatens your family, it needs more detailed examination.

1. Homosexuality Is Caused By A Defective Upbringing. It's The Parents' Fault.

I'd heard somewhere that if the family was somehow neurotic it could case the children to turn out gay, so when Jennifer told us that she was a lesbian, I immediately thought: what's wrong with our family? Was it because I, or her father, had been too influential in her life? I thought back to her childhood and I couldn't think of anything that I had done that might have caused her to be gay. I didn't encourage her to play football or other tomboyish things, although she did tend to seek out boys as her companions rather than girls. At the time we thought it was cute that she was such a tough little cookie, but we certainly didn't push her into these kinds of pursuits. She was never interested in dolls and prams or ballet lessons, she showed more aptitude for cars and woodwork. I suppose we should have realised that these were signs that she wasn't like other girls, but we just assumed she would grow out of it. And anyway, I don't see what we could have done to make it different — we couldn't force her to be interested in cooking and sewing. We had to let her find her own

interests and pursue them. Still, when she first came out,
her mother and me were tormented by the idea that we had
caused Jennifer to be a lesbian by something we had done,
or maybe something we didn't do.

Even though it has been discredited, the theory that some children
turn out to be gay because of a "faulty" upbringing by their parents
hangs on tenaciously in many people's minds.

The most commonly expressed version of this theme is that
homosexual men come from families where the mother is a strong,
overbearing and domineering influence, while the father is weak,
submissive and often absent. Conversely, lesbianism is said to
occur in families where the mother is passive or absent and the
father the dominating figure. This idea seems to have been given
some kind of authority after it was propounded in a study by Irving
Bieber et al, published in 1962 (*Homosexuality: A Psychoanalytic
Study*: Basic Books). Modern researchers dismiss this theory as
being biased by the attitudes of the times and based on inadequate
and poorly controlled research methods (for example, all the
subjects taking part in the study were already in psychoanalysis, so
are unlikely to have been representative of society at large).

A much more authoritative study was carried out at the Kinsey
Institute for Sex Research, and was published in 1981 (Alan P.
Bell, Martin S. Weinberg and Sue K. Hammersmith, *Sexual
Preference: Its Development in Men and Women*: Indiana
University Press). The research methods used in this second study
were far more wide-ranging and convincing, and they showed that
family background has much less influence on the development of
a homosexual orientation than previously imagined. The authors of
this study conducted over fifteen hundred in-depth interviews to try
and discover a common factor in the upbringing of homosexuals
that was different to that of heterosexuals. But no such factor was
found: most gay people came from normal households and had
conventional relationships with parents and siblings. A key
passage in the book says:

> For the benefit of readers who are concerned about what
> parents may do to influence their children's sexual
> preference, we would restate our findings another way. No
> particular phenomenon of family life can be singled out, on
> the basis of our findings, as especially consequential for

either heterosexual or homosexual development. You may supply your sons with footballs and your daughters with dolls, but no-one can guarantee that they will enjoy them. What we seem to have identified...is a pattern of feelings and reactions within the child that cannot be traced back to a single social or psychological root; indeed, homosexuality may arise from a biological precursor (as do left-handedness and allergies, for example) that parents cannot control. In short, concerned parents, we cannot recommend anything beyond care, sympathy, and devotion that good parents will presumably lavish on their children anyway.

One of the twentieth century's most successful literary figures, Christopher Isherwood lampooned the strong mother / weak father theory by saying: "I have been perfectly happy the way I am. If my mother was responsible for it, I am grateful."

2. Some People Are Homosexual Because Of An Imbalance Of Hormones Or For Genetic Reasons.

So, why are some people gay and others not? If it isn't the way they were raised, is it because of a biological factor — is it genetic or hormonal?

There is no positive proof yet available that there is any genetic "cause" for homosexuality. None of the supposed discoveries in this field have remained unchallenged. Experts in the field are unable to agree, and contradict each other constantly. Take these two opinions, the first from Professor Raymond Goodman of Hope Hospital, Manchester in *The Guardian* newspaper:

There is increasing evidence that genetic and hormonal interactions in the developing foetus play some part in shaping sexual, cognitive and behavioural patterns in the future adult. Not only can many of the male and female differences in cognition and sexuality be explained by these processes, but aspects of variant sexuality e.g. homosexuality, have been elucidated. Having individuals with such differences enables a much wider plasticity of thought and behaviour, which in evolutionary terms cannot but be beneficial.

Dr John Bancroft of the Centre for Reproductive Biology in Edinburgh, doesn't agree:

> The determinants of sexual orientation are still obscure. There is no evidence from either primates or humans that sexual preference is innate. Recent attempts to explain homosexual orientation as a consequence of endocrine abnormality during foetal development have not stood up to close scrutiny.

Other recent studies have pursued the idea that homosexuality is a phenomenon decided by genetic factors. One, by the American scientist Simon LeVay, claimed that there was a tiny, but significant, difference between the hypothalamus of gay men and that of straight men. Other researchers claim that they have found a small but measurable difference between the fingerprints of homosexuals and those of heterosexuals. None of this has been proven beyond doubt, and many working in the field treat such findings with great scepticism.

Most rational people would come to the conclusion that sexual orientation is finally determined by an infinitely variable combination of genetic, environmental, social and other factors, none of which we have been able to precisely pin down. We can say with certainty that none of these factors are really under the control of parents — how can we control and change things that we can't even define? Every theory about the development of homosexuality is flawed by the fact that there are thousands of gay individuals who don't fit the formula. For instance, at Tufts University in Massachusetts, research was done into how often homosexuality occurred in pairs of brothers. 167 men and their brothers were studied, split into three groups: 56 pairs of identical twins, who develop from the same egg in the womb and thus share the same genes; 54 pairs of fraternal twins, born simultaneously from separate eggs and as genetically similar as any siblings; and 57 pairs of adoptive brothers who had nothing in common genetically. The scientists discovered that the more genetically similar each subject was to his brother, the more likely he was to be gay himself. 52 per cent of the identical twin brothers of gay subjects were also gay, compared with 22 per cent of fraternal twins and only 11 per cent of adoptive brothers. This report concluded that "the genes men inherit may account for as much as 70 per cent probability that a man will be gay."

This might seem to settle the issue, but another study of twins carried out at the University of Minnesota seems to have reached a different conclusion. A report of this in *The Observer* newspaper said: "In the case of female twins in which one of the pair grew up to be lesbian, the other was always found to be heterosexual. In male twins, however, a few pairs were found in which both were homosexual...This could be coincidence or it could imply that homosexuality in men has a more complex causation."

If, indeed, there is a factor in the way children are raised that has an influence on their eventual sexual orientation, we don't yet know what that it is, and therefore we can't change it. At the moment, it's all guess work.

It is illogical for parents to blame themselves for their child's sexual orientation: no amount of regret, worry or remorse is going to make your child into a heterosexual and no amount of self-blame or guilt will change the situation. So give yourself a break. It's not your — or anybody else's — fault!

The foregoing should also go some way to contradicting the opinion, sometimes put forward by those who consider homosexuality a "sin", that gay people perversely choose to be gay, and therefore can choose not to be gay. All it takes, say these critics, is an effort of will or maybe even prayers to stop being homosexual and start being heterosexual. Such thinking puts enormous pressure on gay people, and on those who love them. Research has shown convincingly that while behaviours might be chosen, basic sexual orientation is not. Failure to recognise the difference means that some gay people spend much time, sometimes their whole lives, struggling to shake off an innate part of their personality. It damages them mentally and denies them the sharing of love and tenderness. Listen to this from Mary, the mother of a twenty-five-year old gay son:

> I was convinced that Howard was doing this on purpose, to be 'diffcrent' in some way. I kept saying to him, 'When are you going to stop all this nonsense in and get yourself a girl friend and settle down?' I used to pile on the guilt, and he'd come back to me saying he was trying to be normal, he was going out with girls, but he didn't really enjoy it. In the end he said: 'Mother, I'm not playing at being homosexual. I

am gay and I really can't do anything about it. I'm wasting
my life trying to find a way out.' In fact, he'd found a
boyfriend and moved in with him. I must say, over the next
few months he seemed happier than I'd seen him for a long
time, and although I was very disapproving at first, I began
to see that maybe this was the best thing for him. After all,
it's his life, and he really had tried to do it my way and
failed. So, I thought, maybe I'd better try and go along with
his way of doing things.

3. Homosexuality Is A Mental Illness In Need Of Treatment.

When I found out about my son Ken, the first thing that
occurred to me was: he's sick in the head, he needs to see a
doctor. I thought that a psychiatrist might be able to
persuade him out of being that way. I tried to persuade him
to go with me to see our GP, so that he could be referred to
a shrink, but Ken wouldn't have it and refused to go.

A lot of the early research into homosexuality was done by
psychiatrists and psychologists using subjects who were already
receiving psychiatric treatment. In those days, when homosexuality
was illegal and completely frowned upon, it would have been
almost impossible to find gay people from the community at large
who were willing to take part in such researches. Naturally, if your
study group is drawn from prisons, mental hospitals and other such
institutions, it's easy to reach the conclusion that homosexuality
itself is a mental illness or delinquency. In those early days of
psychiatry there was as much social pressure on psychiatrists as
anyone else to tow society's moral line, and it would have been
difficult indeed for anyone to produce evidence that contradicted
the deeply-held disapproval.

The approach to homosexuality in those oppressive days was to
devise treatments aimed at "curing" it. One such treatment was
aversion therapy, which consisted of showing the gay person erotic
pictures of their own sex and then giving them electric shocks or
emetics to "turn them off" their sexual preference and, presumably,
on to the opposite sex. None of this was successful in the long
term. People who were given these rather brutal and cruel
treatments did, indeed, feel a lessening of sexual feeling for a
while, but after the treatment ended their feelings returned in their

homosexual form. Thankfully aversion therapy has fallen out of fashion and psychologists and psychiatrists are more inclined to help gay people adjust to and accept their sexuality rather than try to "cure" it. Indeed, one report by Mark Freedman, which was published in *Psychology Today* (March, 1975) asserted that "Homosexuals May Be Healthier than Straights". Freedman compared a group of lesbian women with straight women and found that the lesbians often functioned better than their heterosexual counterparts. The lesbians tended to be more candid and less defensive, had a high degree of adaptability and often reported a sense of freedom.

This new enlightenment was helped along when, on 15th December, 1973, the American Psychiatric Association removed homosexuality from its diagnostic list of emotional disorders. This was followed in 1975 by a statement from The American Psychological Association which said, in part: "Homosexuality *per se* implies no impairment in judgement, stability, reliability, or general social or vocational capabilities." Although there is a small reactionary element in the psychiatric profession which is trying to reverse this, the majority of therapists now accept that homosexuality is not in itself a morbidity.

This does not mean, of course, that homosexuals cannot suffer from mental illness, in the same way that anyone else can. John G. Gonsiorek studied all available research relating to homosexuality and mental illness and concluded that there was no evidence to suggest that homosexuality was, in itself, a pathological condition, but:

> This is not to say that psychologically disturbed homosexuals do not exist; nor does it mean that no homosexuals are disturbed because of their sexuality. Rather, the conclusion is that homosexuality in and of itself bears no necessary relationship to psychological adjustment. This should not be surprising; heterosexuals disturbed because of their sexuality fill many therapists' caseloads.

The conclusion seems to be that while a majority of gays are well-adjusted and content, a sizeable minority are deeply unhappy. But is it homosexuality that is to blame for this unhappiness, or the way straight people treat it? If you want to ensure that your child is not burdened with the "mentally ill" label (which, unfortunately in our society still carries a profound stigma), then you should do your best to relief them of the burden of stress and unhappiness that comes from being unnecessarily at odds with those they love most.

4. Homosexuals Are Lonely, Unhappy People Who Often Commit Suicide.

This idea of homosexuals as sad, rejected victims clings on from the days when it was a justified image. Before homosexuality was partly legalised in Britain in 1967, most gay people had to be very circumspect about their feelings. Any suggestion that individuals might be gay could have had calamitous social and legal consequences — blackmail from criminals or a prison sentence from the law. Before the second world war it was common for gay men to be arrested and imprisoned and to face severe social opprobrium for even minor sexual peccadilloes. Women were regarded as distinctly odd if they did not marry, and many — maybe even most — lesbians *did* follow the convention and entered into heterosexual matrimony, where they were distinctly unhappy. A vivid portrayal of what it was like to be gay only twenty or thirty years ago can be found in the 1960s film *Victim*, which starred Dirk Bogarde as a lawyer being blackmailed because of his homosexuality, or in Quentin Crisp's autobiography *The Naked Civil Servant*.

Under these intense pressures, it was not uncommon to find people with homosexual feelings trying desperately to escape their wretched lot in life. Suicide was one possibility.

Fortunately things have changed considerably in the last few decades, and now gay people are discovering that their lot in life is not necessarily to be miserable and lonely. Many have taken full advantage of the new climate of understanding, and are living full and happy lives. A large-scale survey into the lifestyles of gay men, called Project Sigma, asked of its gay subjects: "Do you regret being homosexual?" 67.1 per cent said "not at all" while 28.7 per cent said "very little" and only 1.8 per cent said "a great deal". Heterosexuals are often mystified about this: why would anyone choose to be a member of a stigmatised minority? Gay people often report that their straight friends asked them: "If there was a pill available that would make you straight, would you take it?" And they are amazed when the majority answer "No". Most gay people have never known what it is like to be any other way, so there is no way they can make sense of such a question, except in terms of convenience and convention. On an emotional level, it is meaningless to them.

But not wanting to change their sexual orientation is not the same as coming to terms with it. It is still difficult for young gay people to find the kind of reassuring information they need in order to develop into better-adjusted adults. Schools are still very cagey about including mention of homosexuality in their sex education programmes and, as we've seen, there is still a lot of negative imagery around to confuse and dismay young gay people. Often young gay people at school are taunted and teased by their contemporaries. Those who don't manage to find friends who can support them through their crisis of doubt and apprehension — so common in teenagers and young people — may become despondent and depressed. Their confusion might also lead them into other antisocial activities such as vandalism, drug taking or prostitution.

Such unsupported (and sometimes persecuted) young people might come to think that suicide is a reasonable way out of their dilemma. Repeated attempts at suicide which fail (called *parasuicides*) are often, as most people recognise, a cry for help. Sometimes gay young people will make a half-hearted attempt to kill themselves as a means of "coming out". The reasoning is that if they can't tell their parents about their homosexuality in words, then the suicide bid might bring the problem to the surface in a way that will force parents to take it seriously.

A few years ago The London Gay Teenage Group conducted a survey of four hundred young people who had defined themselves as homosexual. They found that one in five had attempted suicide because of unhappiness with their sexual orientation. These findings are backed up by an American study conducted by Bell and Weinberg in the 1970s, which found that nearly one in every four lesbians and one in every five gay men surveyed had attempted to kill themselves at least once during their life. Among heterosexuals, the numbers were about one in ten men and one in thirty women. Roughly one quarter of white gay people who attempted suicide were driven to their first attempt by the time they were seventeen; the proportion was even higher for black gays. Well over half of those attempting suicide for the first time did so, they indicated, for reasons of unhappiness concerning their homosexuality; and the problems of trying to fit into a hostile world. A more recent piece of research, published in the journal of the American Academy of Paediatrics (June 1991), showed that 30 per cent of gay men in the USA, between the ages of 14 and 21, had tried to kill themselves.

This was the experience of one mother I spoke to:

My daughter Helen had suffered bouts of depression on and off for about ten years. When she was eighteen she took an overdose of sleeping pills and ended up in hospital having her stomach pumped. I felt desperately sorry for her, but didn't know how to help. I asked her if there was anything I could do, but she wasn't very communicative. I was at my wits end trying to think of ways to get her out of this cycle of depression. Then, a few months later, she took another overdose, and this time, after she recovered, she was referred to a psychiatrist. She told him that she was a lesbian, but that she didn't know what to do about it. She asked the psychiatrist if he would tell me, as she didn't have the courage to tell me herself. This he did. He thought a lot of Helen's trouble sprang from her inability to accept herself as a lesbian, and all the guilt she felt was driving her to these desperate measures. When she came out of hospital and I was able to talk to her, I told her that I really didn't mind, and I was so sorry that she'd kept it bottled up all this time. I said I would try to help her, and I wrote to an agony aunt on a magazine, who gave me some help line numbers to call. I was able to put Helen in touch with these people who helped her enormously. She is now much happier and has a circle of lovely friends — most of them lesbians. If only we could have done this earlier we could have saved her so much misery. In a way I feel bad about not guessing what the trouble was, but I suppose I was waiting for her to tell me. It still makes me shiver to think that one of those suicide attempts might have succeeded and I would have lost one of the best daughters you could ever wish for.

5. There Aren't Many Homosexuals, So What's All The Fuss?

The idea that homosexuals represent only a tiny minority of the population is a very reassuring one for those people who are uncomfortable with the thought of homosexuality. If there aren't many of them about, why waste time thinking about it?

Such escapism is of no use to the parents of lesbians and gays. Even if there were only one homosexual in the world, it still wouldn't excuse the persecution and discrimination that exists.

With the possible exception of the disabled, homosexuals are probably the largest minority in the country. The reason that the myth of the tiny minority has continued is because homosexuals can hide themselves so easily. Unlike immigrants from other cultures who have distinct racial characteristics which make them easy to pick out, homosexuals have no such distinguishing characteristics and so are difficult to identify. They occur in every section of the community: in every class; age group; culture and occupation. Far from fitting the stereotypes of effeminacy for men and masculinity for women, homosexuals are actually, in the main, indistinguishable from the rest of the population. The fact that the vast majority of them choose to "pass for straight" (as failing to challenge the assumption that they are heterosexual is called) adds to the illusion that there aren't many homosexuals.

The familiar kind of flamboyant gay man, portrayed by such comedians as Julian Clary, John Inman, Kenneth Williams and so on, is regarded as "the norm" for homosexuals, because, mostly, they are the only ones who are immediately visible. It was once said that if every gay man and woman in this country were to develop a green nose tomorrow, the whole issue of homosexual discrimination would be ended immediately, because then it would be apparent that we all know, and love, lots of homosexuals and were never even aware of it.

As more and more gay people get the confidence to come out, the popular idea that all gay men are effeminate becomes harder and harder to sustain. It may be fun to have a "camp" comedian on TV, but it shouldn't be thought that such people represent gay men as a whole. There is no "average" gay man: they come in all shapes, sizes and kinds.

This is not to say that there aren't effeminate gay men and butch gay women, or that their needs are any the less important.

Such people do exist, and we'll look more closely at their needs a little later.

So, how many gay people are there in Britain?

It's a very difficult question to answer with any accuracy. The first serious survey into the incidence of homosexuality in Western societies was carried out in the United States by Dr Alfred Kinsey and his colleagues at the Kinsey Institute for Sex Research. Between the years 1938 and 1963 the Institute gathered nationally representative data, drawn from many thousands of interviews, on the incidence of homosexuality among American men and women. The survey showed that roughly one in three men and one in five women have had at least some overtly homosexual experience between their teens and middle age. For many of them, that experience had been more than incidental. Nearly 21% of white, college educated men and 7% of white college-educated women report having had sex with two or more persons of their own gender and/or having gay sex six or more times. Percentages for non-college white men and women are 28% and 5% respectively. Black people reported fewer incidences of gay sexual experience — only 16% of black college men and 3% of women. Across the board, gay men seem to outnumber gay women by three to one. No one knows why this should be.

But, of course, simply having one homosexual experience (or even several) doesn't necessarily mean that a person is gay. The Kinsey Institute also produced a continuum of sexual behaviour — which runs from zero to six, to indicate the degree of homosexuality or heterosexuality that a person has in his or her personality. Zero indicates that a person is entirely heterosexual, and has never had a homosexual experience, while six indicates that a person is completely homosexual, with no heterosexual experience. Along the line — where most people are situated — there is a mixture of "largely homosexual, but with incidental heterosexual history" (5 on the scale); "largely homosexual, but with a distinct heterosexual history" (4 on the scale); "equally heterosexual and homosexual" (3); "largely heterosexual, but with a distinct homosexual history" (2).

The latest research was carried out in Britain in 1993 and published as *Sexual Behaviour in Britain - the national survey of sexual attitudes and lifestyles* (Penguin Books, 1994). A cursory reading seems to indicate that of the 20,000 Britons chosen at random to be questioned, only 1.1 per cent of the male respondents had had a sexual partner of the same sex over the past year. But this needs to be qualified. As the authors of the report say, the figures should be regarded with extreme caution and be seen as only very conservative estimates. Also, of the people who had been approached to take part in the research, over 40 per cent had refused. This led one commentator to write: "Imagine you are a gay teacher, army officer, Tory MP or a married man with a gay lover. Would you be part of the 60 per cent (who took part) or the other 40 per cent. And if you join the 60 per cent, would you tell the truth? All of it?"

The old figure of 10 per cent which was bandied around for so many years was obviously incorrect. But it is highly unlikely that one per cent is accurate either.

6. My Child Must Have Been Seduced Into Homosexuality By An Older Person

> When Don came home from college and told us that he was
> a homosexual and was moving in with another man, I said
> to him: 'This other man, he's put this idea into your head,
> hasn't he? I told you to watch out for people like that.'

As we've already discovered, homosexual orientation is fixed long before people are aware of what is happening and before anyone can do anything about it. The idea that sexual preferences can be changed by persuasion is common, but doesn't stand up to examination. Imagine it the other way round: if you're straight, could someone persuade you to be a homosexual against your will? When looked at it in those terms, we can see how improbable such an idea is.

Those who want to stand in the way of progress for homosexuals often say that all teenagers go through a "homosexual phase" and that if it is discouraged (or at least not actively encouraged), it will pass. The argument then goes on to say that if children are given positive information about homosexuality during this period of supposed sexual confusion, they will turn into "permanent" homosexuals. This was this reasoning behind Britain's notorious Section 28 of the Local Government Act, which prevents local authorities from "promoting homosexuality" in schools.

However, there is much misunderstanding about what is meant by this "homosexual phase." While it is true that many young people at school are curious about their burgeoning sexuality, and often seek to explore it with members of their own sex, this cannot really be said to be setting the seeds of a "permanent" gay personality. It's often nothing more than simple curiosity.

Similarly, when young girls begin to moon over their female teacher or when boys feel strongly drawn to their male teachers, it often seems to express itself in a sexual desire. Any counsellor or teacher will tell you of the desperate pleas for help received from young people who say they have fallen in love with their teacher, or with some other adult authority figure. These feelings have been called "puppy love", "teenage crushes", "hero worship" and so on, and when seen as a part of adolescent development — the need for admirable role models — rather than some sinister homosexual plot, they seem far less serious. They should not be seen, though, as justification for believing that a gay child will "grow out of it." Being curious about other people's bodies (and how they are developing in comparison with your own) is very different from having the distinct feeling that you are "different" in a much deeper way. So, we must be careful to bear in mind that sexual identity and sexual behaviour are not necessarily the same thing. Naturally adults who take advantage of any confusion felt by young, immature people are to be deplored, but it is unlikely that even that kind of exploitation could entirely change the course of a person's sexual orientation.

Those young people who define themselves as gay — sometimes even before they have engaged in any homosexual activity — must be taken seriously. They may be aware that their fantasies and desires are consistently directed at members of their own sex. They know that their inner sexual identity is not the same as that of their friends, even though they may not possess the vocabulary to name their feelings. This is quite different from having an occasional exploratory sexual experience with a friend who happens to be of the same gender as yourself.

If young people have recognised that they have a gay identity even before they have had sexual experience of any kind, then it is highly unlikely that anyone is going to change them. Similarly no-one can seduce young heterosexuals into believing that they have a gay identity if that isn't the case.

The researchers Reiche and Danneker, of Frankfurt University, conducted a large-scale study of nearly 800 homosexual men, and said:

> In our empirical study...we could show that about 30 per cent of subjects had their first homosexual experience before the age of 18, and they involved a partner who himself was not older than 18. Only 34 per cent of our subjects had their first homosexual experience with a partner before the age of 18 with a partner who was aged 18 or over. Apart from the fact that there is no such thing as seduction into homosexuality, it is also clear that another common supposition is wrong; the supposition that the first homosexual experience would take place between an older man, supposed to be a homosexual, and a juvenile...This initial thesis that the genesis of homosexuality can be attributed to seduction by adults is, therefore, empirically wrong.

The authors of *Sexual Preference: Its Development in Men and Women* found that there was a significant period of time, in most cases, between a young gay person becoming aware of their sexual preferences and their acting on them. It is clear, therefore, that the vast majority of younger gay men and lesbians know about their sexual orientation long before they have any sexual experience.

This also pours cold water on the theory that older gay men and women spend their time seducing youngsters into homosexuality. Even when older people do seduce younger people (and in the vast majority of cases it is heterosexual men who pester young girls), it is unlikely that basic sexual orientation would be affected. Young heterosexual boys who have been subjected to homosexual abuse (often by their own fathers or other members of the family), have not gone on to become homosexuals themselves. Although the abuse may well have had a detrimental effect upon the child, it would not turn him into a homosexual if he weren't already homosexually inclined.

In passing, it is important to mention that homosexuals are also burdened with the reputation of being child abusers. Home Office statistics, however, show that about 98 per cent of child abuse is carried out by heterosexual men against girls. Much of the abuse of boys is also carried out by heterosexual men: it seems that the sex of the child is often unimportant to those who are drawn to such activities.

Homosexuals should not be confused with paedophiles (adults who are attracted to children for sexual gratification). Although there are some homosexuals who are also paedophiles, it is proportionally no more than the heterosexual population.

7. Homosexuals Are That Way Because They Had A Nasty Experience With The Opposite Sex.

I would say to Daniel, 'You used to have girlfriends in the past. Why did you stop seeing them? Did something happen that put you off women?'

Swaggering straight men will often say to gay women: "You wouldn't want to be a lesbian if you'd let me show you what it's like with a man." Like the anxious mother quoted above, they are labouring under the impression that gay people have, somewhere along the line, had a bad experience with the opposite sex which has turned them away from heterosexuality and toward homosexuality. The truth is more likely to be that relationships with the opposite sex failed because the gay person was trying to be something he or she couldn't be.

Gay men don't, as a rule, "hate women", and gay women don't generally "hate men" (although sometimes they'll say they do as part of a political statement). Indeed, some gay men relate marvellously to women and many women love their gay friends dearly. Often they feel "safer" with gay men because they don't feel sexually threatened.

Just because gay men and women don't want to make their romantic relationships with members of the opposite sex, doesn't mean they hate them. If you watch your gay son or daughter relating to people generally, you'll see that he or she responds in much the same way as anyone else does, judging people on their personal qualities rather than their gender.

Trying to force people into being something they just can't be, is asking for conflict and disappointment.

8. Lesbians And Gay Men Like Dressing Up As The Opposite Sex

The popular images of gay men and lesbians usually include some element of cross-dressing. Cartoonists who want to portray lesbians will show them dressed in tweeds, wearing a monocle and smoking a pipe. If it's gay men they want to lampoon, there will inevitably be a handbag, high-heel shoes and lurid make-up. But is this a true picture? Do lesbians and gay men feel a compulsion towards transvestism, as dressing in clothes of the opposite sex is called?

The answer is that some do, but most don't. "Drag queens" are very popular as entertainers in gay venues, as they are in many other places. The idea of men impersonating women has fascinated people over the ages and "drag" has been popular for many centuries and in many cultures. The panto dame is a great British tradition which foreigners often find bewildering. Lily Savage, the classic gay drag queen, has become a popular and well-loved entertainer with audiences far beyond the gay pubs in which he started his career.

But beyond the professional entertainers, there are actually few homosexuals who are into cross-dressing. The fact that the ones who are interested in it have such a high profile, and the ones who aren't are so invisible, gives an unbalanced picture to the casual observer.

On the other hand, items of clothing traditionally associated with men have become popular with some lesbians. Heavy boots, tailored trousers, ties and short-cropped 'masculine' hairstyles are worn by some women as a challenge to the "role" they have been expected to play.

Clothing has also become, in the gay community, an important means of expression. Young people especially experiment with clothing to create different images of themselves. Many of these experiments have filtered out into the wider community and it is not uncommon these days to see in the High Street, clothing 'statements' which originated in the gay community (men wearing earrings, torn jeans as a gesture of defiance, leather jackets and trousers as macho symbols etc.). Society's attitude to clothing is changing more radically. Men are increasingly wearing brighter and more flamboyant clothes, and there is a less rigid demarcation between what is acceptable and what is not for the sexes to wear. But many parents still worry that because, as a child, their son dressed up in mum's clothes occasionally, it somehow made him gay.

There is no doubt that the way some gay youngsters choose to dress is a source of conflict with their parents. The October, 1988 issue of *Gay Times* carried the story of the Ward family from Leeds. Bob and Doreen Ward's teenage son James came out to them after some consideration. James tells of how he tried to let the world know about his homosexuality without actually saying it, by changing his appearance.

> Before reaching the stage of 'coming out' to himself, James expressed his sexuality by more indirect means. Never interested in the same things as his peers at school, he developed a talent for 'unmanly' pursuits, becoming one of the most successful Avon sales representatives in Leeds and he took up a cultivatedly camp appearance, wearing his hair long and his face plastered in makeup. 'It was the only way I could express myself. I felt very isolated and needed an identity, without coming out as such. If somebody at school called me 'queer' and I was walking around being as camp as Christmas, they couldn't really get at me.' This strategy — a kind of double-think where homosexuality is simultaneously admitted and denied — was followed by James' full acceptance of himself and, interestingly, once he came out, he cut his hair, stopped wearing makeup and dropped the camp affectations.

Fathers become uncomfortable with what they see as 'pansified' clothes, and constantly criticise their son's dress sense. Lesbians are often the butt of nasty remarks and disapproval because they dress to please themselves and their friends rather than their family. But parental criticism of their children's clothes is not limited to homosexuals — most young people use clothes as a means of asserting their individuality It is just that fashions among gay people are usually one step ahead of the mainstream, and their challenge to strict gender rules is discomfiting for many people.

It's not likely that a childhood interest in dressing up would have affected your child's sexual orientation, but some researchers have suggested that boys who show an exclusive interest in feminine things during their childhood may well be giving an indication that they are growing up gay. Hopefully, though, this knowledge will not be used as a rationale for preventing children expressing themselves in their own way. Attempts to force children into playing games that they hate or taking up activities that don't interest them is a recipe for later rebellion. Some fathers, for instance, might insist that their son join the school rugby team, even though the child would be happier in the music society or drama group. Mothers might force their daughters into domestic science lessons, even though the girl would prefer woodwork or car maintenance. Attempts to force the child into what the parents consider 'normal' activities are doomed to failure The pattern of their sexual preference is likely to have been set by the time it becomes apparent through behaviour. Insisting that a child suppresses his or her natural talents and interests in the interest of conventionality is cruel and unfair.

Transvestism is actually much more common among heterosexual men than it is among homosexuals. On the problem page at *Woman's Own* we would have many letters every year from married men who felt a compulsion to wear their wives clothing. They did not consider themselves homosexual in any way. Their interest in women's clothes is seen as an expression of their heterosexuality — by putting on their wives' underwear, these men are attempting to get closer to women, not further away. And when they had got over the shock of discovering their husband's preferences, the wives were often sympathetic. Most regarded it as a harmless eccentricity rather than a serious sexual problem.

9. Homosexuals Are People Who Have Been Born Into The Wrong Sex

This confuses homosexuality with transsexuality. Some people genuinely do believe that they have been born into the wrong sex, and stories about sex-changes (or gender re-assignment) are quite common in newspapers. However, the people who consider themselves to be a man in a woman's body, or vice versa, are not usually homosexual. Many of them have led conventional, heterosexual lives, fathering (or mothering, in the case of female-to-male transsexuals) children. However, the pressure they feel about being born into the wrong gender leads many of them to seek medical help and, eventually, a surgical change.

Some transsexuals find their way into the gay community not because they are gay, but because this is one place where there is an element of understanding and acceptance.

10. *Living A Homosexual Lifestyle Is Unhealthy*

This idea has taken on a new significance since the advent of AIDS, but I can do no better than to quote from an article by Dr John Bancroft of the Centre for Reproductive Biology in Edinburgh, which appeared in *The British Medical Journal* (No. 6644):

> AIDS is not a homosexual disease, but in the Western world, and in the United States in particular, male homosexuals have born the brunt of the epidemic. One consequence has been a vigorous reappraisal of homosexuality...Doctors have a long and dubious tradition of influencing sexual morality under the guise of medical wisdom. In the past non-procreative sex, such as masturbation, has been proscribed on the grounds of causing serious illness and even insanity...In general doctors have colluded with the process Barbara Wootton described as 'the concept of illness expanding at the expense of the concept of moral failure.' It is questionable which label, 'sickness' or 'sin' does more harm to the well being of homosexuals. Most doctors now accept that there is no rational basis for regarding homosexuality itself as an illness. A homosexual lifestyle is compatible with all the criteria of health except possibly fertility — and voluntary infertility is not regarded as an illness. Illness can be manifested as sexual behaviour, but such behaviour is more likely to be heterosexual than homosexual.

11. *Homosexuals Can Look Forward To A Miserable, Lonely Old Age*

Some of them can, but so can many heterosexuals. That has more to do with society's attitudes to old age than with sexual orientation. However, a survey of the lives of older gay men was published in America (Berger: *Gay and Gray*, Alyson Publications, 1982). It revealed that there was little difference between the psychological and physical development of homosexuals and heterosexuals. It concluded:

> Although the death of friends and family is a burden shared by older heterosexuals and homosexuals, the older homosexual is less likely to invest himself entirely in a single spouse. The issue of widowhood or widowerhood is therefore less salient in the gay community. There are of course many instances where two homosexuals men have invested themselves in a relationship lasting many years; the death of a partner is then a serious life disruption for the man who remains. But the homosexual, aware of his isolation at an early age, is perhaps more likely than the heterosexual to have developed strong friendship bonds, and these friendships are then a resource in crisis situations.

A similar pattern was observed in a study of gay women (*Lesbians Over 60 Speak For Themselves*, Monika Kehoe, Harrington Park Press, 1990). This survey found that although gay women were more prone to loneliness and financial insecurity in their old age than were gay men, they remained well-adjusted:

> In spite of their advanced years, their physical and emotional health is good, and they score in the upper percentiles on the Life Satisfaction Scale. The large majority feel positive about their lifestyle and even about ageing. This outlook manifests a well-being that puts these women in a rather special category.

The people who took part in these two studies came, of course, from a generation in which homosexuality was severely punished. It is miraculous that they have managed to reach their old age in such fine emotional fettle. The next generation of older gay people will find a very different society. The gay community is better organised, and already provision is being made in a small way for the needs of elderly homosexuals. Special sheltered housing and old folks homes are being planned. The prospects for having a happier gay old age look better now than they have ever done.

These are only a few of the misunderstandings that stand in the way of your accepting your gay child. We'll look more closely at some of the others in subsequent chapters.

Having gleaned some of the facts and figures from authoritative sources, it becomes clear that homosexual people are unfairly labelled and misunderstood. But why do these myths continue, when they are so obviously untrue? The awful fact is that it is in some people's interest to sustain the idea that homosexuals are pariahs and outcasts.

Over the past few years homosexuality has become a hot topic in politics and in the church (and just about every other social institution). Right-wing politicians and religious leaders have realised that the fear and misunderstanding which surround homosexuals can be manipulated to their own advantage. Many unscrupulous politicians have tried to use gay people as a means of attaining and retaining power. They have manipulated the deep-seated homophobia of our society, and tried desperately to reinforce the untruths that are widely believed. The tabloid press has conspired in this manipulation with a daily diet of condemnatory articles and features.

When thinking about this, bear in mind that your child is included when people in politics or in the churches issue blanket condemnations of homosexuals. Next time you read some sordid stereotype being peddled about homosexuality, remember that not only does it damage your own child, it damages millions of others, who feel unjustly isolated and abused.

This is what one mother of a gay son had to say:

My son had told us that he was gay about two years ago, and I had not mentioned it since then, preferring to keep it quiet, hoping it would go away. During that time I began to notice how much was being written in my daily paper about homosexuals, and almost all of it was uncomplimentary.

I became very upset every time I read one of these stories about famous male personalities having boyfriends or some group demanding grants from local councils. Every time some politico said 'It's disgusting and unnatural' or something like that, I'd shrivel up inside and die a little. I used to think: 'Where is all this hatred coming from?' and how on earth could it all be to do with my own son? I was worried about the kind of people he was mixing with, because I knew he wasn't like the way they described it in the paper. So one day I went round to his flat to see him.

I wanted to raise the subject. Until then he'd respected my wish not to talk about it, but it was getting on my nerves so much, that I just had to ask him what was going on. He answered all my questions honestly, and I came to realise that maybe there was another side to the story. I stopped worrying about the awful things that were being said about gay people in the papers. I still don't talk to him much about what goes on in his life, but I know I could if I wanted to.

These myths and misunderstandings hurt real people, and it is important that they are challenged. I hope that what you've read — and what you'll go on to read — will go some way to helping you see that your there are other ways of approaching these problems, and all is far from lost.

Empathy Is The Keyword

Empathy is defined in the dictionary as "power of projecting one's personality into (and so fully comprehending) the object of contemplation." In the sense that we want to use it, it means putting yourself into the shoes of your gay child, and trying to feel for yourself what he or she must be feeling. Stop for a moment and try to imagine what it would be like if you were gay. What if everyone thought that you fitted the terrible, untrue stereotypes that we have been discussing? Imagine living in constant fear that your family might withdraw their love and support from you at a moment's notice. Imagine being the object of ridicule and hatred for something completely beyond your control.

Your child might have borne such fears for a long, long time. He or she is likely to have kept them bottled up over an extended period, living in constant apprehension that someone would "find out". It is a secret that he or she would be unlikely to have shared with anyone but the most trusted friend. Not very pleasant, is it?

Now your child has gathered the courage to free him or herself from the burden of secrecy. It may have taken several years before they could risk disclosure. Try to empathise: imagine the trepidation that must have led up to the moment when the announcement was made. Think about the terror of taking the plunge and then waiting for the reaction: would the family still love and support you, or would you be thrown out into the street and completely rejected? Would those people, who mean most to you in the world, understand, or would they despise you?

If you have projected yourself into that situation for just a moment and visualised how it must have felt, then it will have done both of you a favour. For now you should have a small insight into what is happening and why it is happening. It will be further food for your subconscious mind as it progresses in its search for a solution to your distress.

3.
Keeping it in the family

So where do you go from here? You now know that you have a lesbian daughter or a gay son, and you are working on your feelings about that, but what about other people? How will other members of the family take the news — indeed, how many of them already know? What will the grandparents say? Or the extended family? Or the neighbours? You may fear that this revelation will split your family from top to bottom, and lose you the regard of your friends and colleagues.

The boot is now, in many ways, on the other foot. Your child has made his or her decision to come out and, in doing so, has handed the initiative to you. It's now your turn to decide whether to tell those who are important to you that your child is gay.

The question is: if you decide to share this secret with other people, who will they be? Would it help you to talk to your best friend, or do you dread rejection? Will you feel better if your own parents know about their grandchild, or don't you think they could take it?

The immediate reaction of many parents is: "Don't tell anyone else, let's keep it just between ourselves." This is what writer George Weinberg identified as a conflict between two "parenting themes": a love theme and a conventionality theme. The 'love theme' compels parents to accept their children as they are, regardless of social values. Parent-child love and loyalty take precedence over society's demands for conventional behaviour. The 'conventionality theme', on the other hand, compels parents to demand that their children live by society's rules and regulations, and censure them if they don't. In most cases, the love theme eventually gains the ascendancy and a new, more realistic image of the homosexual child is constructed by the parents, even though it contradicts society's ideas of what is normal. Parents must work out for themselves how that emotional about-face will be achieved.

In the early stages of the parents' conflict, it is likely that heavy demands will be made on their gay child to keep the "shameful secret" away from other people. It is reasoned that this is the only way to protect the family's reputation in the eyes of the community. However, having taken the difficult decision to come out, the gay person might be determined to complete the job by telling at least selected other people. This was Marjorie's experience with her son, Michael.

> I didn't want Michael to tell his father. I knew it would cause big problems. But Michael was equally determined that not only was he going to tell his dad, but his brothers and sisters, too, and then his grandparents. I had visions of the family falling apart, because I had the feeling that some of our relatives just wouldn't be able to handle it. There is a strong religious streak running through parts of my husband's family, and I thought this would be very difficult for them to cope with. I told Michael that I would never speak to him again if he went ahead and told everyone. I was very angry with him, almost hysterical at times. I was sure the family would disown us.

Against his mother's wishes, Michael did tell the rest of the family. They all took it fairly well, no-one showed signs of being unwilling or unable to cope, although there was an element of shock from some quarters. Marjorie then said:

> When he'd done it, I couldn't stay angry with him. In a way I was glad, because now I didn't have to worry about them finding out in some other way. And I could talk to them about how I felt and how they felt. Michael's brother was very good about it, taking the news very matter-of-factly. In a strange way that helped me: because he was so calm, I felt quite melodramatic in comparison. Michael's father, on the other hand, went very quiet. He hasn't properly talked about it yet, and whenever I try to raise the subject he just clams up and refuses to respond.

Brothers and sisters: their right to know

Research has shown that brothers and sisters (siblings) often play a very important part in each other's development. They frequently act as "sounding boards", helping each other develop a sense of identity and intimacy. Brothers and sisters who are reasonably close to each other in age, will spend a lot of time together testing out ideas and discoveries about life on each other. By gauging the reaction of a brother or sister to various life events, youngsters gain a sense of what is important and what is acceptable, and this helps them enormously in creating a realistic self-image. With this in mind, it is natural that when a young person discovers he or she is gay, they may want to share the realisation with their siblings; this might be the only sure way they know of testing the validity of their feelings. Consequently it is quite common for gay young people to come out to their brothers and sisters before they tell their parents.

Brothers and sisters can also act as a support when the day comes to make the revelation to parents. I have spoken to many gay people who first came out to their siblings and then, when they told their parents, called on the brothers and sisters to act as allies. There was an element of that sibling support mechanism in Marjorie's story above. In isolated instances there may be two gay people in the same family. If this is the case each will be able to provide a unique support system for the other but, perhaps, a double shock for the parents.

Sometimes, brothers and sisters can be less than supportive. Sibling relationships are often complicated by other considerations and many parents will know only too well the rivalry and love-hate element in some sibling friendships. We all know brothers and sisters (in whatever combination) who are, in many respects, inseparable and loyal, but are in other ways, remarkably cruel to each other. The revelation of homosexuality in younger siblings might lead to one using it as a weapon against the other. Parents should be wary of this. Homosexuality might become a useful tool of manipulation to settle some other, unrelated, score. Indeed, during the "mourning period" which follows the announcement, some siblings can feel resentment at what they see as neglect from their parents, who seem to be using all their emotional resources dealing with the coming out crisis.

Not all brothers and sisters react with enthusiasm or understanding to the news of their sibling's homosexuality. One researcher into this (C. Jones, *Understanding Gay Relatives and Friends*: Seabury Press, 1978) found that while some parents tended to react with guilt, brothers and sisters sometimes reacted with anger and confusion. Young people, particularly adolescents who are struggling with their own sexual identity, are afraid of the social consequences of their brother or sister's coming out. Adolescents have a strong need to feel that they are accepted by their 'pack'; they often dress similarly, like the same music and gather together at the same social events. This sharing of attitudes and tastes reinforces their group identity. Many siblings of newly-come out gay people are afraid that their peers will imagine that they, too, may be gay. If still at school may be anxious that the news does not reach the ears of their contemporaries, lest they should be somehow judged guilty by association.

This is what Barry, 16, had to say about his gay brother, John:

> I wasn't particularly upset when John told me he was gay. I just thought it was his own business, and I didn't really feel any different towards him — he was still John, even if he was a fairy. But I was a bit worried that it would get round at school. There's already a lot of ragging goes on about queers, mostly just in good fun, but it gets to you when you know somebody who's gay. I didn't want anybody to think that I was gay, though, and I begged John not to mention it at school so that it wouldn't be an issue for us. He agreed not to tell anyone except his best friends, and so far it hasn't got round the school generally. I don't think I'd like it if it did. It might ruin my chances with girls.

Some parents worry about what to tell very young children in their family. When is it appropriate for them to know? Naturally this will be an individual decision for each family, but a rule of thumb could be "when they can understand." They will naturally pick up charged atmospheres and attitude-changes at home. If they aren't let in on the secret, they may feel excluded from full participation in family life. The authors of a book called *Counselling Lesbian Women and Gay Men: life issues* (A.E. Moses & R.O. Hawkins, V. Mosby & Co.), found that younger children tend not to react to homosexuality with quite the same ferocious negativism as adults.

This is probably because they haven't taken in society's prejudices and disapproval and they don't yet know how society expects people to behave sexually.

One counsellor of the parents of gay people found that in some instances the confused parents thought that they should stop their gay child sleeping in the same bedroom as their brothers or sisters. Rose Robertson says, on this subject:

> To separate without explanation, and for no logical reason, two brothers or two sisters who have previously shared a bedroom is unnecessary and wrong. The homosexual brother or sister will inevitably feel rejected by and under suspicion from their own family.

There is certainly no need to feel that such action is necessary: homosexuality is not 'catching' and, as we've already found, no-one can be persuaded into being gay. There is no danger to your non-homosexual children, but such thinking might well hurt your gay child immeasurably.

The Extended Family

When all the immediate family know about your son or daughter's homosexuality, you then have to make a decision about the rest of your extended family. Much will depend on how you get on with them, of course, and how close you feel to them. Most of us have family members who we just don't care for, and whose opinions aren't really important to us. But others, you might feel, need to know. If the family is to function honestly, then you have to consider coming out perhaps to your own parents or to cousins, aunts, uncles, nieces and nephews.

After a few months of thought and worry, Marjorie had decided that she wanted to tell her mother about Michael's homosexuality. Michael and his grandmother had always been close, but since the revelation he had been reluctant to go to her house. Marjorie's husband, Will, had urged Marjorie not to do it:

> Will kept saying that my mother was too old to understand and that she wasn't strong enough to take it. I didn't agree, as my mother has always been very open about things like that. I was just sorry to see her and Michael drawing apart

from each other. I asked Michael if he minded if I told mother, mainly because I wanted someone I could trust to talk to about it. He said it was all right, so I went along to her house for a cup of tea. She took it ever so well, didn't bat an eyelid, whereas I wept buckets. I've been able to talk to her about all the fears I've got about Michael, and although she would prefer it if he wasn't that way, she says she still loves him and will stand by him if there's any trouble in the family. She still wants him to come and visit her. He was very relieved when I told him, and he's been round to see her a couple of times since then. I feel much, much better for having told mother, and she's been a great help and comfort to me.

It's commonly thought that old people, like children, should be protected from bad news wherever possible, but this is simply patronising. In their research paper *Ageing and Wisdom; Individual and Collective Aspects,* two doctors specialising in the elderly (S.B. Brent and D. Watson), said that older people are more likely to take the news with equanimity than younger or middle-aged people. They said that life experiences often gave older adults extra insight or wisdom into personal relationships, social values and decision-making. This extra insight and knowledge of social bonds — and what can go wrong with them — could well moderate the reactions of older persons to homosexuality in the family. It might be thought that because they were raised in a time when homosexuality wasn't talked about, they don't know anything about it. This is nonsense — homosexuality has always been around, and although it may not have been a topic for general discussion in the early part of the century, it certainly has been since. Older people, like everyone else, have been exposed to the explosion of media interest in homosexuality, especially since the AIDS crisis developed. They, too, may share the generally negative opinions of homosexuality but, like you, they will be motivated to work on them when someone they love is involved.

There is much evidence to suggest, also, that same-sex members of the family are likely to react badly to the revelation of a person's homosexuality. A lot of fathers will not take the news of their son's gayness quite as well as mothers do, and mothers will generally find it harder to cope with their daughter's lesbianism. There is another division here, in that women fare much better on the whole than men in dealing with this whole question. You will have noticed that the testimonies of fathers in this book are few and far between, and that is because men are less likely to want to think about their child's sexuality in positive terms. Often they simply refuse to discuss it. If there is to be a bad reaction, it most often comes from the father. A possible explanation for this was offered by Richard Ashworth, a lawyer and president of the New York chapter of the Parents and Friends of Lesbians and Gays group. He thinks that:

> Fathers do have different expectations for their children. We train males to be macho. So being "he-man" is a very important thing. Fathers may expect to live their lack of success in that area through their children. I think you may find more disappointment in a father at first. I don't think you find that as much in a mother. Mothers don't have those expectations.

This is not universal, of course, and many fathers cope marvellously with their gay child, acting as a support and friend in difficult times, while mothers may go to pieces completely. There are no accurate ways to predict how a person will cope.

Sylvia has a lesbian daughter, Sandra, who is at college. She came out to her mother in a letter. This gave Sylvia time to think about the issues before Sandra came home for the summer holiday. She felt able to welcome her daughter back with open arms and they talked for many hours about what this all meant to them. Sylvia had shared the news with her immediate family on the same day that the letter came. She felt she had no right to keep it from them, and so Sandra's father and her two brothers also knew. The whole immediate family had been supportive, and they had refused to treat Sandra as in any way different. But now Sylvia had to decide whether she was going to tell the rest of her family. She has a close friendship with two of her cousins and sees them often. She decided to invite them over and tell them about Sandra's letter:

> My cousin Lena was most understanding. She read the letter and said 'Well, it's not such a big deal these days is it? And Sandra's still the same girl that we've known and loved all these years.' She made me get the photo albums out of the cupboard so that we could look at some of the old

pictures we'd had taken when we were all on holiday together. There was Sandra, as a little girl, building sand-castles with Lena's kids. I remember that holiday very well, we all got on like a house on fire. It all seemed so normal — you'd never guess from looking at that carefree little girl playing on the beach that she was a lesbian.

My other cousin, Angela, wasn't so reassuring. She sat there very quiet while all this was going on, so in the end I said to her: 'What do you think, Angie?' And she said: 'I don't want to be offensive, Sylvia, but I find it very difficult to understand. Has she been influenced by somebody at college? You never know who they're mixing with when they go away from home. I think you ought to bring her out of that college and keep an eye on her. It isn't right, it isn't natural. You ought to discourage her before it goes any further.'

Lena was furious with her. 'What do you know about it?' she said, 'What makes you such an expert? This is Sandra we're talking about, not some stranger who we don't care for. I think you ought to find out a thing or two before you start spouting off. After all, look at your David, always in trouble with the police — he's hardly a marvellous example of good behaviour, is he?' Angie was angry and went home in a temper.

After she'd calmed down a bit, Lena told me that her own son was gay, and that she hadn't told anyone because she was afraid they'd react like Angela — or worse. The trouble was, she felt she'd dealt with it so badly that she'd driven her boy away. He'd moved to London so he could have a life of his own away from the pressure of his family. She was very sad that they'd drifted apart on such bad terms, and now that she'd had time to find out more and think it through, she just wishes she could get her son back and tell him how much she loves him and misses him. She didn't want me to make the same mistakes with Sandra. I was amazed, and we had a lot to talk about.

Sylvia had found, quite by chance, a person who had shared her own fears and doubts, and the two of them were able to support each other through difficult times.

If you aren't lucky enough to find support within your family, you can always consider talking to a counsellor (carefully chosen to ensure that he or she knows what they're talking about and aren't likely to make things worse) or a member of a parents-of-gays support group. You'll find a list of them in the back of this book.

Reading and educating yourself from books about the facts of homosexuality is important, but there is no substitute for talking to someone about your own particular situation. This is where your own coming out can be such a great comfort (as well as a risk).

In an article in *The Guardian* newspaper, Liz Hodgkinson wrote about the telling of secrets:

> Most of us have secrets of some kind, things we would rather other people didn't know about and that we try to hide from the rest of the world — and sometimes from ourselves. Yet the paradox is that when eventually it comes out, there is often an overwhelming feeling of liberation; one no longer has to live a lie, terrified that someone will discover the truth.

In the same article a psychotherapist, Vera Diamond, is quoted as saying:

> Keeping a shameful secret is like locking up a wild animal behind a steel door. It's always knocking and scrabbling at the door, trying to get out, and you're terrified it will — so you keep working to make the door safer and more impenetrable. The effect is isolation and fear. You imagine you are the only person in the world with such a dreadful secret, that everyone else is nice, normal and happy. You feel out of touch with the world...And as the years go by and the secret remains hidden, an enormous fear barrier builds up and your whole being becomes devoted to keeping the secret locked up. Only when it does come out can things get back in proportion, as you realise you are not alone — there are thousands of other people who share your problem. From then on, your whole life does not have to be wrapped around the secret and the guilt vanishes.

Vera Diamond believes that today's climate allows us to unburden ourselves more easily of many of the secrets we feel are "shameful." The plethora of television programmes devoted to social problems, and the subsequent increase of understanding of a whole range of what were once taboo subjects, ensures that at least people will have heard the topic discussed before, even if they haven't thought about it in depth.

Often you will find that friends and relatives will be more than willing to offer the support you need. A problem is diminished once it is shared.

Beyond The Family

Avril has a lesbian daughter and wanted to share this secret with her best friend Brenda. The two women were very close and confided in each other to a great extent. Eventually Avril took the plunge and told Brenda about it — the first person she'd come out to:

> Brenda was an absolute rock. She calmed me down and helped me to get the whole thing in proportion. She was always cutting articles out of magazines for me or telling me when relevant programmes were coming up on the television so that I wouldn't miss them. I was hungry for information, and she made sure I got it. She even went with me to a meeting of this Parents of Gays group that I'd found. I don't know what I would have done without her. I've been able to look at Cheryl in a completely different way since Brenda helped me along. We've even been to Cheryl's flat, which she shares with her girlfriend, and although I felt a bit uncomfortable at first, I've got over that now and we're all back together as one big happy family. I can't tell you what a relief it was to be able to tell Brenda and have her on my side.

Although she got a wonderful, helpful reaction, Avril had still been worried that she might lose Brenda's friendship. She knew already that Brenda was an open-minded and well-informed woman, but Avril's own distorted feelings of guilt and shame had caused her to imagine that everyone else felt the same way. In the end, she got everything she had hoped for from her friend — a constructive and knowledgeable ally. Unfortunately, not everyone is as clued-up and supportive as Brenda, and sometimes it is better to find expert advice and support than to rely on friends whose knowledge of homosexuality might be even less than your own. The myths we've already discussed are deeply planted in many people's minds, and in seeking help from ignorant friends you may be asking to have your distress increased rather than reduced.

If you decide to go for trained or specialist help, make sure you ask some pertinent questions of any potential counsellor before committing yourself. Any counsellor worth their salt will help you explore your feelings and thoughts about your gay child without any kind of pejorative or judgmental reactions. If he or she is sensitive to what is needed, your course of counselling should result in your being able to discard your old ideas of what you thought your child was and embrace a new understanding. Your counsellor should be able to help you articulate and criticise your existing values, some of which you will never have faced before. You may need to redefine some of these values in the light of new information, and to help you do this, you'll need unbiased facts. Hopefully this book will have provided some, but there will be other things you'll want to talk about, too. Your counselling should help you gain a clearer perspective of the role your child's sexuality plays in his life. After all, it isn't the totality of his or her character, and shouldn't be allowed to completely dominate your opinion of your child's value as a whole human being.

The importance of checking the credentials of those from whom you are seeking help is illustrated in the experience of one mother of a gay man:

> I didn't know where to look for help and in the end I decided to go along to my doctor. I just couldn't think of anyone else. He was very censorious, and said that I should do my best to persuade my son out of it. The doctor was a fairly old chap, quite near to retirement. He said that it was probably a phase and that if my son was still claiming to be a homosexual in a year's time, I should bring him in to the surgery and the doctor would see about referring him to a psychiatrist. He also said my boy should have a test for AIDS. When I came out of the surgery I was more upset than ever. Looking back on that visit to the doctor, I realise how bigoted he was in his approach, and I can't imagine why I took any notice of him. I found out a lot more about homosexuality since then, and I realise that my GP didn't

really know what he was talking about. I've always been raised to respect doctors, and I found it difficult to refute what he said.

The prejudice and misunderstanding about homosexuality is so deep-seated that even those who have been well-educated can still subscribe to the mythology. Attitudes are changing fast in the caring professions, but there are still pockets of ignorance; be wary of them.

As your son or daughter will tell you, there is no real formula for coming out successfully; it's less a one-off event, more a continuing process. Each time you meet someone new, to whom the knowledge may be relevant, you have to decide whether you are going to tell them. Gay people are faced with this dilemma throughout their lives to tell or to keep quiet. As we've already seen, in most instances they keep quiet! The same principle applies to you. Do you tell your colleagues at work or do you think it is irrelevant? Do you want to share the news with your circle of intimates, or do you think there's no reason for them to know? Your opinion on this topic will change as time passes and as you continue to work on your feelings.

Sometimes the choice is made impetuously, sometimes only after long and hard consideration. In Marjorie's case the problem came up at work when she heard someone making offensive anti-gay remarks. She wanted very much to say something, to show her displeasure at what was going on, but knew that if she did, she might well be letting the cat out of the bag about her own daughter. In the end she made a general remark about prejudice and bigotry, showing her disapproval of the anti-gay remarks without committing herself. In other instances she might well have had to justify her stand. What if her colleagues had challenged her: "Why should you care whether we talk about lezzies and nancy-boys?" How would she have responded — with the truth or with a cover-up? Similar situations will arise for you from time to time, and each decision will be unique to that occasion.

Avril, whom we met earlier, eventually reached the stage of feeling that the persecution of gay people was unfair and unnecessary. She wanted to defend her daughter when she was under attack, and she wanted to protest when gay people in general were being defamed. One of her colleagues asked her what she had planned for one particular weekend. Avril had replied that she was going to visit her daughter in her new home. "Is she living alone?" the colleague had asked. "No," Avril had replied, "She's living with her girlfriend, and we'll all be going out for a lovely meal together on Saturday night."

> She was dumb struck, but I felt great. I'd done it at last! I knew it would get round on the factory grapevine in no time, but I didn't mind. I felt strong enough to cope with it and justify my support of my daughter. I loved her more than any of the people I worked with, and so I felt it was right to be loyal to her. I was surprised at myself, but proud as well. I'd reached the point where I could stand with Cheryl whatever the circumstances. When I think of some of the terrible things that might have happened to her in life, I don't suppose being a lesbian is all that terrible. She's got a lovely home with her girlfriend Kath, and they have the kind of lifestyle other people would envy. When I think of the torment I went through, I can honestly say that I feel happier now than I have done for a long, long time. I'm ashamed of some of the things I've thought about her, and how I've imagined all kinds of rubbishy things were going to happen to her. Now I've got her and Kath, and you couldn't imagine any two people you'd rather have in your family.

Coming out to your family and friends as the parent of a gay child may be stressful, but it helps in many ways. Firstly, you can get the support and information that you need so desperately. Secondly, it relieves the burden of secrecy that often hangs over a home when only some of the family members know. A great barrier can arise which casts a shadow over all family relationships, creating distress and worry for those who know something's going on but not what it is. Thirdly, it will enable you to move on through the previously mentioned stages of acceptance. It will reinforce your determination to come to terms with the situation and help you create a more honest and realistic image of your son or daughter. It should be possible for you to get some positive input to help you along.

It's important to retain your dignity throughout this whole procedure. Try not to project a feeling of shame or apology on to those you tell — it might affect their own reaction. If they're taking their lead from you, they could pick up your fears and begin to share them. As for those more distant friends, and those who don't need to know as a matter of urgency, it might be as well to keep things to yourself until you feel comfortable to tell the news in a more knowledgeable way. Once you've calmed down, and have a little more information at your disposal, you can tell the less significant people in your life with more confidence and less fear.

Marriage problems can be intensified

It is often noted by counsellors and others who offer help to parents in distress, that the coming out of their child can precipitate or magnify other problems in the marriage. Difficulties which have been left unresolved in the partnership can become major issues when this extra burden is placed upon the family. This is particularly true if sexual problems exist between husband and wife. As Rose Robertson puts it:

> A parent with sexual difficulties of any kind will tend to assume that this has been the cause of the child's homosexuality. Careful and patient counselling is essential in these cases, and frequently leads to areas of difficulty for the parents far removed from the original issue, the young person's homosexuality.

The gay child should not become the scapegoat for pre-existing problems between the parents. It is unfair to blame a gay child if the relationship between his parents disintegrates or becomes difficult after the disclosure of homosexuality. It is more likely that the extra pressure has brought other, previously unspoken, grievances to the surface.

Some couples have reported that the coming out crisis actually brought them closer together. They faced the problems as a couple and felt a new sense of partnership as a result. This was what happened to Jane and Eric when they found out their son was gay:

> After John told us about himself, both Eric and I retreated into ourselves for a while. We grew apart and found it very difficult to talk. But after a while we started to realise that we just couldn't remain in this miserable, non-communicating condition any longer and so we sat down

and spoke openly about how we felt. It was a great relief, and we came up with some positive suggestions about what we ought to do. I felt the depression lifting from me after I was able to share it with Eric, and strangely enough we started talking about other things, too. It was as though we had opened up lines of communication that we hadn't previously had. We've stopped worrying about John now, and he's getting on with his own life. We don't interfere, but we do take an active interest. John doesn't have a partner yet, but we live in hopes that he'll find whatever it is that he wants before much longer. In the meantime, our own lives have taken on a new vigour.

To summarise:

• Parents have their own coming out to consider: when is the right time to tell, and who are the people who need to know?

• Brothers and sisters can be a great support, but they can also feel excluded from participation in the family if they aren't told. You can gauge what their reactions might be by looking at their present relationship with their gay brother or sister: if they got on well before they knew, they're likely to take the news well. If there was friction and distance between them, then it's likely they won't react so positively. Younger people — particularly adolescents — might be undergoing their own identity crisis, which might cause them to react in unpredictable ways.

• If your child is close to his or her grandparents, they shouldn't be excluded either. Remember, it's likely that older people will probably take the news better than you did! Once again, pre-existing attitudes might be an indicator of what reaction you can expect, but nothing is certain with this particular topic.

• Friends can provide a great support in times of doubt and distress: but make sure you can trust your confidantes, and make sure that any advice they give you is based on knowledge and not ignorance.

• If you can't get support from your family or friends, find a qualified counsellor who is sympathetic to your plight. Find them listed in the phone book or ask your doctor for a recommendation. Ask a few pertinent questions of any therapist before undertaking a course — is the counsellor properly qualified; is he or she well-informed on the subject of homosexuality; is he or she going to point you in the direction you want to go?

• Coming out, in however limited a way, will help you enormously in relieving the pressures of secrecy and guilt. But you may want to wait until you feel better and calmer about the whole subject before coming out to those who don't urgently need to know.

• Remember to try at all times to empathise with your child's plight. By having to keep his or her secret, you will have experienced something of what he or she has had to endure for many years. Always bear in mind that whatever set-backs you experience along the way, ultimately the goal is to improve the quality of your family life.

• Keep a sense of proportion: remember homosexuality is only one aspect of your son's or daughter's personality, admittedly an important one, but it's certainly not the be all and end all. Despite the fact that he's gay, your son will retain all those other personality traits that made him so loveable — if he was a great practical joker before, he will remain so. If your daughter was good company when you felt lonely, she will be still. Your child may be brilliantly academic or skilled in some practical way, he or she may be musical or otherwise creative. Whenever I've counselled distressed parents, I've always ask them to think back to the time before they knew about their child's sexuality, and to remember some act of kindness or thoughtfulness their son or daughter had done for them. One mother said she was grateful to her daughter for arranging a surprise party for her wedding anniversary, another said her son always helped with any decorating or repairs that needed doing in the house. Yet another said her son had used his professional skills to help her get out of a tricky situation with the tax-man, while one just said she was grateful that her daughter was such a good friend.
Make an effort to think about the many talents and gifts your child might have, however modest they might be, and don't turn

him or her into a two-dimensional stereotype. He or she is not *just* a homosexual, but a hundred other things as well.

• If your child specifically asks you not to tell anyone else, how do you cope with other people's direct questions? One response could be to say: "Ask him/her yourself." That gives your child the opportunity to make their own decision as to whether they want to come out to that particular individual.

4.
Friends and lovers

If your son or daughter has taken the momentous step of coming out to you, it is likely that he or she has already made other gay friends, or will be trying to do so. When parents think of this, it immediately sets up yet another conflict in their mind. If the child is still living at home, the first question is – should I encourage, or even allow these friendships? The reasoning goes something like this: If I let him have gay friends, will they persuade him to be even more gay? If I keep him away from them, might there still be a chance that he'll change?

If your son or daughter is an independent adult living away from home, then the question becomes: should I accept or condone these friendships? It just seems like another nail in the coffin of your hopes and expectations.

The other reason parents resist their children's gay friends is because they imagine that their own off-spring is an exception to the rule. Although parents may have tried to challenge the preconceived ideas of what gay people are like, a residual doubt may still linger. ("My daughter is fine – I can just about live with the news that she's a lesbian, but surely she's different from the others?") Immediately all the old fears are conjured up. "I don't want him mixing with all these dreadful, maladjusted individuals that you hear so much about" say some parents. But the old canard that my-son's-OK-but-he's-an-exception just won't wash with young gay people nowadays. You may think that the gay world is populated entirely by sinister ne'er-do-wells, but your son or daughter knows differently. Most homosexuals do not fit the mould into which they've been forced. They aren't all sex-obsessed monsters or pathetic creatures with nothing to recommend them.

As you are beginning to discover, most homosexuals are indistinguishable from the rest of the population. You're probably already well acquainted with several very respectable gay people, even though you may not be aware of it. And if you try harder to challenge the ready-made ideas of what "they" are like, you may well be pleasantly surprised to find that your son or daughter is socialising with a group of pleasant, well-adjusted people who will, if you let them, happily come into your life and quite possibly enrich it.

That, in itself, is a generalisation, of course, and there are some bad homosexual people, just as there are bad heterosexuals. You must make your assessment about their worth as you come to know them, but you should try very hard not to judge on the basis of their sexuality before you've even met them.

Remember this, written by Dr Wayne Dwyer in his book *Your Erroneous Zones* (Sphere Books, 1977):

> Rigidity is the basis of all prejudice, which means to prejudge. Prejudice is based less on hate and dislike for certain people, ideas, or activities than on the fact that it's easier and safer to stay with the known. That is, people who are like you. Your prejudices seem to work for you. They keep you away from people, things and ideas that are unknown and potentially troublesome. Actually they work against you by preventing you from exploring the unknown. Being spontaneous means eliminating your prejudgments and allowing yourself to meet and deal with new people and ideas. Prejudgments themselves are a safety valve for avoiding murky or puzzling provinces and preventing growth. If you don't trust anyone you can't get a 'handle on,' it really means you don't trust yourself on unfamiliar ground.

One mother, Irene, found this out for herself, in relation to her 17-year old son, Andrew:

> Andrew started bringing friends home very soon after he told us he was gay. I don't think he realised that we were still reeling from the shock, and then to bring other homosexuals into the house was a bit much. But as I met the other boys he knew, I gradually accepted that they were very much like Andrew – same age group, same interests and always polite. One of them, Gareth, had been coming round

to our house since he was a child, and I had realised that he and Andrew had spent most of their childhood together. I felt relieved that they had each other to lean on. Their friendship will probably see them through the rest of their lives, and that makes me very happy. Although Andrew says that he still hasn't found a 'boyfriend' and that all the people he knows are just friends, I'm still not comfortable with them going up to Andrew's room together, and I usually make them stay downstairs where I can see what's going on.

Derek and his wife Karen live in a Midlands town. They have a thirty-year old gay son, Richard, who lives in a council flat near to his work in the town centre. Derek and Karen quite often go round there to visit, and over the years they've come to know many of Richard's friends. Richard feels comfortable enough with his parents to invite them to parties and social events at his home and they feel secure enough to go. Here's what Derek said:

I have to say that it's never been much of a problem accepting Richard for what he is. I never felt I had to condemn him. In fact, it was quite interesting. We continued going round to his flat to visit, and we found that he had a whole network of friends, men and women, who he had never told us about. Most of them were great, and we've increased our own social circle. In fact, we've become so friendly with some of his mates, that they come round to visit us independently. It never occurred to me to think of them as homosexuals or lesbians or anything else, they were just people who I either liked or I didn't like, depending on how we reacted to each other. I can understand how some parents can be nervous, but Karen and me have always been good mixers, and we welcomed the chance to be part of our son's life. We don't feel cheated, we feel privileged.

Mr or Ms Right

Like any other human being, your gay child is likely to want to have a close and loving relationship with another human being. And now we're getting down to the real nitty-gritty difference between what you thought your child was and what he or she actually is.

I imagined I was over the shock of finding out about Glenys being a lesbian, but then one day she rang up and said she'd met this girl and asked if she could bring her round to meet us. It was a bit of a setback for me, it was like hearing the news all over again. I had no idea that she was seeing anyone, I had the impression she was living on her own. I said it was OK, but I started to feel uneasy as soon as I'd put the phone down. My husband was OK about it, he said he didn't mind, but I was getting more and more agitated as the time came round for them to arrive. I lost a night's sleep worrying about what I would say to this girl and how I would cope with knowing that they were probably having sex together. I was grateful that they wouldn't be staying the night, because then I would have had to worry about what the sleeping arrangements would be. That's the thing that was really troubling me.

Accepting that a child is gay on an intellectual level is quite different from acknowledging what it might mean in practical – and sexual – terms. When your beloved daughter or son announces that they're setting up in a relationship with someone of the same sex, the whole thing takes on a reality that you might have previously denied. Any remaining thoughts you might have harboured about your child having made a mistake in identifying himself or herself as gay will have to be abandoned. If you'd hoped that it was only a phase, then you'll now be seeing those hopes dashed. All the troubling thoughts about sexual activity come marching back to the front of your mind. This is it, the real thing.

Of course it doesn't always work this way round, sometimes your child will wait until he or she has found someone special before deciding to come out to you. Until that time they've probably imagined that telling you the truth would just be an unnecessary hassle. But now they have a partner who will support them through the crisis, they may feel more confident to come out to you. If things go wrong, he or she won't be on their own with the problem.

More likely, though, your son or daughter might simply want you to recognise and approve the relationship. After all, it's important that those who play a significant role in our life should know important things about us.

The First Meeting

Vera is a widow living alone in a provincial town. Her son, Tim, moved to London some time ago to take up a job. He's kept in touch with his mother over the years, more from a sense of duty than from any enthusiasm. Vera feels that since Tim moved away they had lost the closeness they had previously shared. Vera had little idea of the kind of life Tim was living, because he didn't seem inclined to tell her about it. She had simply hoped that he was comfortable and happy.

> About four years ago, Tim rang me and said he was coming home for a visit, and could he bring a friend with him, as he had something to tell me. I had no idea what sex this friend was going to be, and when they arrived Tim said: 'Mum I want you to meet Peter. We're going to live together. We're gay.' And there stood this young man, a total stranger, looking sheepish and worried. I was a bit knocked back, but I was polite, and I made a cup of tea for the three of us and we had a good old chat about the whole thing. Peter turned out to be a very nice young man, well-mannered and very sensible. I said to them: 'I don't suppose there's much else to say. I hope it will work out for you.' Naturally I want Tim to be as happy as he can be, and if that's the life he wants, then who am I to interfere? He is an only child, though, and I was a bit disappointed that there wouldn't be a wedding or in-laws or grandchildren.
>
> After that, Tim started to ring me a lot more regularly, and eventually he asked if I would like to go and stay with them at this new house they'd bought together. I was a bit worried about it. I didn't know whether I could cope with seeing the two of them together, and thinking of them sleeping in the same bed. I thought I'd be embarrassed, seeing two men living like a married couple; it seemed so unnatural. But he was persistent, and eventually I said OK, I'd go. When I got there, it wasn't anything like I'd imagined. Their home is beautifully kept, but then Tim has always been a tidy soul, and they've got a dog and a cat. They couldn't have been more welcoming, and they did everything they could to make me comfortable. Peter is a good cook, so we had some

nice food, and wine with the meals. This loosened my
tongue a bit, and I was able to ask Peter the kind of question
I wouldn't have if I was entirely sober. He was very
forthcoming, and said that he loved Tim, and hoped that
they'd be together for a long, long time. I must say, they
both seemed very happy together, but even so, I went to bed
that night and had a good cry. I should have been glad for
them, but I suppose I was crying for myself, and everything
that I thought I'd lost. No grandchildren, no big family. I
had to get it off my chest. But after that, I came to see that
the life they were making for themselves was just as good as
anything else. It's no use wishing things were different,
because they can't be and it's taken me a long time to realise
that. I still love Tim dearly, and I've got a soft spot for Peter,
too. He always remembers my birthday and mother's day
and things like that. I feel much closer to my son now than I
did before he told me all this. And I know if I want to, I can
go and stay with them whenever I like. I don't feel as lonely
as I did before.

May parents have reported that they had great difficulty accepting
the idea of their child living in a relationship, even though they
wanted him or her to be happy. Those who broke down the barrier
far enough to actually meet their child's partner were often
pleasantly surprised, and subsequently came to like their child's
partner very much, often integrating him or her into the family.

Sometimes the gay child does not come out at all in the formal
sense, but simply assumes that the parents know what the situation
is. This is the case with Valerie and Dave and their son, Gerry.
Valerie explains:

Gerry has lived on his own in a flat for some time. He
seemed quite happy, as it wasn't very far away from us.
We've always been close, so we thought we knew a lot about
what was going on in his life. He would come round to our
house to use our washing machine, as he didn't have one in
his flat, and to have Sunday lunch with us. We suspected
that he might be gay, but we didn't say anything to him, and
he never volunteered the information. It was just sort of
unsaid. He never seemed to have girlfriends, and he wasn't
very forthcoming about his social life, although he never

seemed to be short of friends. Then one day he said he was moving into a semi-detached house with another chap, Joe. He said it was time for him to go upmarket and get out of that grotty flat. He made out that he was just sharing expenses with Joe, but we knew it was more than that. After all, when two single thirty-year-old men move in with each other, you have to consider it's a bit unusual. We gradually got to know Joe, and found him a very pleasant person. He came round to our house more and more with Gerry, and soon we were inviting the pair of them to family functions. They came to our golden wedding anniversary, and that was a big family do. Nobody batted an eyelid or asked any questions about them. They are just 'the boys' as far as the family are concerned, and we're quite happy with that. There's never been any question of being cool towards them – we're not that kind of people. Gerry is very much loved in our family and always has been. In many ways he's the life and soul of it. I'm just very pleased that he's making such a happy life for himself and Joe.

The situation where everyone in the family knows about the homosexual relationship, but no-one speaks about it, is very common, and it suits some people. There was a famous cartoon which showed a young boy kneeling beside his bed saying his prayers, the accompanying caption read: "...and God bless Uncle Harry and his roommate George who we aren't supposed to talk about."

With this "unnamed relationship" situation, the issues don't have to be addressed and everyone just gets on with it, without hostility or rancour. Why bother making an issue of it, then, some parents might ask. Why not just leave it unspoken and there won't be any embarrassment or need to upset people?

The answer is that some gay people feel that refusing to recognise their relationship for what it is, robs it of its dignity. They want their family to know them not just as "friends" – which suggests a casual arrangement for practical purposes – but a fully committed emotional and sexual partnership. Although it might be easier for parents and family not to have to deal with this fact, many gay people demand it in order to ensure that their relationship is taken seriously.

Sex, Sex, Sex

Many parents find the sexual aspect of their child's relationship almost impossible to deal with. They cannot shake off the idea that this is the final proof that their beloved child really is a "pervert" and abnormal. They are sickened at the idea of what gay people might do together in bed.

Listen to Tracy, talking about her son, Barry:

> I was really trying hard to come to terms with Barry living with this other man. Finally I went round to their flat to meet him. I was having a cup of tea, sitting right on the edge of the chair, feeling extremely uncomfortable. I couldn't get out of my mind just what the two of them did when they went to bed together. As much as I tried, I couldn't stop thinking about it. Then our Barry went to get something out of the bedroom and as he opened the door I caught a glimpse of this double bed. Well, that was it. I couldn't stand it any longer and I just had to make an excuse and go home. It still makes my hair creep a bit, although I am quite coming to like Barry's friend, the more I talk to him.

Many parents report that they find the thought of their son or daughter having sex with another man or woman at best unsettling and at worst totally intolerable. If this is the case for you, then I can only recommend that you make a large effort to put the whole thing out of your mind. To be blunt: it's none of your business. Your son or daughter, as much as anyone else, is entitled to privacy, and his or her sexual activities should be as personal as those of your own – or any of your other children's.

If you find the persistent thoughts of your gay child's love life are interfering with your progress towards accepting their relationship on a broader level, you might like to try a method called "thought-stopping". This technique was invented by an American psychologist as a means of dealing with intrusive, obsessive thoughts. The object of thought-stopping is to replace the tormenting thought with something more pleasant, and entirely unconnected. So, in advance you would make a list of several pleasant mental images which will be used to replace any troubling thoughts about your child's sex life.

Maybe you could conjure up in your imagination a pleasing picture of your holiday – a particular beach, a particular meal, a particular person – anything that does not involve your child. Get this thought or image ready in advance, and when you feel that the undesirable thoughts about your child's homosexuality are forming in your mind, immediately shout: STOP! (you can do this in your imagination if it's not convenient to shout it out loud). Immediately conjure up your pleasant thought to replace the unpleasant one. Do this every time the disturbing thoughts start to creep back, and soon you will have banished them from your mind.

Some people find that having an elastic band around their wrist is useful — they simply snap that instead of shouting STOP! and then conjure up their pleasant thought – and really work on making it a vivid picture in their imagination.

It may seem far-fetched, but in fact it has been proved that if you are systematic about it, this technique does work, and once you've mastered it, you can use it for other obsessive worries that crop up in life. If you practise thought-stopping day-by-day the intrusive and upsetting worries will occur less frequently until you have them completely under control..

But He Was Married...

One mother I met, who was still in a state of confusion after finding out that her divorced son was living in a homosexual relationship, asked:

Why does he want to live like this? He was a normal man, married for more than five years to a lovely girl. They didn't have any children and I was sorry when they broke up, but I accepted it. These things happen – everyone makes mistakes. But then when I found out he was living with another man, I just couldn't understand it at all. I find it very difficult to talk to him about it, even though he's tried to raise the topic with me. I'm quite a strong Christian, and much of what has been taught to me over the years tells me that what my son is doing is wrong. I've asked a lot of questions about homosexuality, and I've learned a bit more about it, but there are still things nagging away in my mind. What does he get from living with another man? They can't have children, they can't ever be part of the community in the same way he was with his wife. And other little things keep troubling me, silly things. Who does the washing and cooking? Who cleans the house? It makes me ill to think of my son acting as a woman. I can't let go of all these doubts, and I haven't plucked up the courage to go round and see him. And I've forbidden his man friend to come and see me and my husband. I'm not sure I could cope with it. I still love my son very much, but I can't accept him in the way that he wants me to.

The kinds of questions raised by this mother are common ones for the parents of gays. What exactly is a homosexual relationship, and how does it differ from a heterosexual one? Perhaps we should start by looking at why gay people need relationships at all.

Homosexuals are raised, in the same way as everyone else, to believe that having an intimate and loving partner is a primary goal in life. For heterosexuals this usually means marriage, and although no precisely equivalent institution exists for gay couples it doesn't stop the desire for a "special someone". As the authors Berger and Kellner put it in their 1975 study *Marriage and the Construction of Reality* (Aldine Publishing Co):

Having to live in the larger society...the adolescent soon feels the need for a 'little world' of his own, having been socialized in such a way that only by having such a world to withdraw into can he successfully cope with the anonymous big world that confronts him as soon as he steps outside his parental home.

This simply confirms what philosophers down the ages have always known – we would have no sense of reality if we did not have other people to confirm our existence. It is only by seeing the reactions of those around us that we can know what kind of person we are. In an intimate, one-to-one relationship this sense of reality can be fully explored. Our partner can come to know us better than anyone else in the world, and wc can come to know ourselves better through that same relationship. By testing out our deepest feelings on our partner, we can gauge whether those feelings are good, bad, noble or unworthy. We can know whether our jokes are funny, or whether we are seen as interesting, loveable or boring. Our partner can bring all these benefits and more.

And so the desire for a close partner – a soulmate, if you like – is deeply imbued in all of us from a very early age, and the urge to fulfil that desire is very strong indeed. Every gay person I have ever spoken to has expressed the wish to have a permanent or semi-permanent relationship, and the motives are the same as for heterosexuals: for love, companionship, caring, and for practical reasons like sharing expenses.

But there are profound differences, too, between heterosexual and homosexual relationships. To begin with, straight couples can usually depend upon the full support of their family and of society at large. Gay couples can expect the reverse: disapproval and condemnation are frequent reactions. Heterosexuals can generally conduct their marriages in the open, able to talk about them and about their hopes and fears for the future. Homosexual couples, on the other hand, often have to be secretive and keep the truth of their personal lives hidden from view; they have to lie about its nature and occasionally even deny it exists.

As with homosexuality in general, a whole mythology has grown up around gay relationships. Erroneous ideas abound, and some of those were expressed by the last mother quoted above. So, before we look more closely at what all this means for you, your child and the rest of your family, let's look at how much truth there is in some of the commonly held misconceptions about same-sex relationships.

Misconception 1. *Gay relationships don't last very long. Gay men are too promiscuous, and gay women are too unstable.*

It's true that sometimes gay relationships don't last very long, but then how long does a relationship have to last before it has any value? Everyone starts a serious relationship – whether marriage or not – with the hope that it will last for a substantial period of time, if not for the rest of their lives. Only a minority stay the course. Let's face it, with the divorce rate running at almost fifty per cent, heterosexuals can hardly claim to be perfect in this department. And how many engagements are broken before the couple reach the altar? Nobody ever says that all heterosexual relationships are unstable just because they frequently come to an end. Only the luckiest among us find our ideal partner at the first attempt. Yet each time a gay relationship hits the rocks, the sages shake their heads and say: "Well, that sort of relationship is doomed from the start." They wouldn't dream of making such a sweeping statement about heterosexual unions, despite the fact that the majority don't last.

With all the extra pressures on their relationships, it's a wonder that gay relationships ever get started in the first place. Just because a relationship doesn't work out doesn't mean that the participants didn't enter into the it in a spirit of good faith.

There have been many theories propounded about the supposed promiscuity of gay men. One of these is that men are generally more easily aroused by purely sexual stimuli than are women. Women place less emphasis on physical arousal and almost always need an emotional element to their love making. Therefore, if two men meet and want to have sex together there are few restraints of an emotional nature, as there would be between a man and a woman or between two women. In these circumstances two men could more easily have a brief encounter that had little other meaning than sexual gratification. This is far less likely between women.

Another element might be the fact that the odds are stacked against gay men meeting in circumstances other than those which presuppose a sexual encounter. As sexologists Bell and Weinberg put it:

> Society provides gays with little or no opportunity to meet on anything more than a sexual basis. Driven underground, segregated in what have been termed 'sexual market places', threatened but perhaps also stimulated by the danger of their enterprise, homosexual men would be expected to have an enormous number of fleeting sexual encounters.

This was written in 1975 at the peak of the sexual revolution and before the AIDS crisis arose. Since then, an enormous education campaign has been conducted within the gay community, warning of the dangers of promiscuous lifestyles, and this message has, in the main, been taken on board. The image of the indiscriminate homosexual is outdated. There are certainly still men who have many sexual partners, but it is more usual now for gay men to be careful and cautious in their sex lives.

The idea that lesbians are, in some unspecified way, "unstable" and, therefore, unable to sustain relationships together over a long period is another myth that doesn't stand up to examination.

Lesbian women are no more likely to be "unstable" than anyone else, indeed, there is evidence to suggest that two women living in a relationship have a head start over a man and a woman. They will place more emphasis on each others feelings, and place great value on fidelity. Research into lesbian couples has indicated that judged on the commitment and loyalty they show each other, the openness and honesty they display, their relationships are generally of a very high quality indeed.

There seems recently to have been much more interest in exploring the idea of long-term relationships in the gay world, and many more gay couples are forming with the intention of trying for longer commitment. Even though there is still a great deal of homophobia around, there is also more tolerance for homosexuals and gay couples are far more likely to find support these days than they have been in the past. There is hope that this new tolerance will help their partnerships become more stable.

Despite all the pressure of disapproval that have attended most gay relationships over the years, many survived and thrived against all the odds. Listen to this gay couple, Darren and George, who are trying hard to make a secure life for themselves that will release them from the need to seek other partners in less than desirable places.

Darren: We don't want to spend the rest of our lives searching in gay clubs and bars for someone we can live with. We're grateful to have found each other, and we're trying hard to establish ourselves as a full-scale relationship. We live together, and share everything. We know that things can go wrong, and we're determined to work on that.

George: We've told our parents and they are fairly supportive, although they still can't accept us on the same terms as they do our married brothers and sisters. Of course, we can't get legally married, so there is no piece of paper that gives our relationship the same legal validity as that of my brothers. But we regard our relationship as the equivalent of a marriage, and we ask people to take it seriously. Most of our straight friends are great about it.

In Edinburgh, Richard and Chris have been living quietly as a gay couple for over thirty-seven years. They met when homosexuality was completely illegal and they had to be very discreet about their lifestyle until quite recently. They first met, all those years ago, in a public lavatory. As Chris says:

> In those days this was just about the only way that gay people could find each other. It was a bit desperate and very dangerous – if you were caught it meant ruin, and maybe even a jail sentence. When I met Richard we realised that we had more in common than just sex and it blossomed from there. We've lived together since then, and we've had a full and happy life. We've both contributed our share to society, having worked in the public service all this time. We also take a very prominent part in our local community life. We don't consider ourselves to be anything special, and we don't get any problem from anyone. All our friends and family are accepting. We don't make a fuss about being gay, and everyone ensures that we're both included in family events. We've had all the same troubles over the years as any other couple that stays together over half a lifetime. We expect to be together now until we die – I just can't imagine what life would be like without him. Nor do I feel that we've missed out on anything. I never wanted children, so don't feel cheated on that score. I'm glad, though, that young people these days don't have to put up with a lot of the nonsense that we had to endure in our time.

Although there is no such thing as a legally binding "gay marriage" in Britain, some Scandinavian countries have given homosexual couples the right to register their relationships at the local Town Hall – which they have been doing at the rate of fifty a month. These contracts give the same-sex couples similar benefits to those enjoyed by their heterosexual equivalents, except that the gay couples cannot adopt children and the ceremony can only be a civil event – there cannot be a church wedding for gay couples. The registrations are only for citizens of the countries concerned and are not recognised outside those countries. Many hundreds of couples in these forward-thinking nations have taken the opportunity to have their relationships legally recognised. Now other progressive countries are thinking of following suit, on the assumption that by encouraging stable gay relationships, they can help cut the incidence of AIDS in their gay communities.

Misconception 2. *They have to decide which of them will be "the man" and which "the wife."*

The idea that gay relationships are simply carbon copies of heterosexual marriage, with a man and pseudo woman, or a woman and a pretend man, is totally erroneous. The popular image of a gay couple as consisting of one effeminate man who stays at home and cleans and cooks whilst the other smokes a pipe and goes out to earn a living, just doesn't hold water. And neither does the idea of a lesbian couple consisting of a butch woman, earning the bread while her compliant "wife" sees to the domestic arrangements. Indeed, gay relationships have an element of equality which is often missing in marriage.

Even in these supposedly enlightened times, men are socialised to behave in a particular way – to be strong, tough, aggressive, with the ability to keep emotions under tight control. Women, too, are raised with certain expectations in common with each other – to be nurturing, caring, emotional, cooperative. There are still very rigid ideas about what constitutes a man's role in life and what a woman's. Only comparatively recently have women begun to challenge the preformed pigeonhole into which they are expected to fit. The stereotyped sex roles are beginning to break down, but only slowly and with a great deal of resistance.

Lesbian women have always been at odds with society because, by following their feelings, they would be forced to reject the idea that women need men in order to get through life successfully. Many lesbian women have been trail-blazers in the fight for women's emancipation and liberation. When two men or two women get together in an emotional partnership, it is likely that both will have similar expectations. Research into how gay couples function reveals that when two males live together they manage to adjust their attitudes sufficiently to be able to share those tasks which are traditionally ascribed to women. They tend to share their domestic and practical duties equally between them. Similarly, women living in a lesbian relationship are not likely to adopt rigid roles that echo heterosexual relationships. They will assign tasks in a way that is equitable, and negotiate their way through the problems of finances, shared property and child care (if this is an issue for them).

Naturally if one member of the partnership is houseproud, it is likely that he or she will do more of the cleaning and dusting. If one of the partners is a better cook than the other, then that is likely to become his or her duty. But generally male couples manage to work out between them an acceptable division of labour that doesn't leave one of them feeling like "the little woman". Similarly, women are less likely to live in the "butch" and "femme" roles that popular culture likes to portray.

Of course, there are as many ways of living together as there are couples, and any combination of arrangements is possible. In some ways this is superior to many heterosexual marriages, because one partner is less likely to feel hard done by or oppressed within the relationship. The "frustrated housewife" syndrome, which leaves so many heterosexual women feeling unfulfilled, is less likely to happen in a gay relationship.

Misconception 3. *Gay relationships don't last because there are no children to hold them together.*

Once more it has to be said that no-one would make such a sweeping generalisation about heterosexual couples who, because of infertility or choice, do not have children. Many married people manage to sustain their love and commitment to each other even though their union provides no children. It would be hurtful indeed to suggest that the marriages of infertile people are meaningless and their love unworthy.

Although the gay couple can't produce children between them, it does not mean that they are incapable of producing children at all. Some parents will be reading this book after discovering that one of their adult children – who has been married and already produced offspring – is gay.

Because of the enormous pressure on people to get married, many gay people still do so. Sometimes they marry to satisfy the demands of a close-knit family, sometimes they do it because they feel that it might make the gay feelings go away, and sometimes they do it because they feel the marriage will give them a protective cover behind which to hide their true sexuality. Whatever the reason, thousands of gay people are, or have been, married, and most of them have been mothers or fathers. What the arrangements are after their heterosexual relationship has broken up vary. This is Nina talking about her daughter, Sonia, who divorced her husband after nine years of marriage and two children:

Sonia told me many years ago that she was lesbian and, indeed, before she married she had several girlfriends. I didn't think much of it at the time, and I wasn't surprised when she came home one day and announced that she was getting married. She lived a reasonably conventional life for the nine years that the marriage lasted, and I have two of the sweetest grandchildren anyone could ask for. When the marriage broke down there was a lot of acrimony and bitterness. Sonia naturally wanted to keep the children, but her husband wanted them, too. However, after they'd had time to cool down, Leo recognised that it would be impractical for him to keep the children as he was away so often on business. They came to an informal arrangement whereby he would be able to visit whenever he wanted and have complete access to them. It was only after a few months that I came to know the reason for the divorce – her name was Erica. Sonia and Erica have set up home with the two kiddies. I was frantic at first, full of troubled thoughts of how the children would find out about their mother and this other woman and what the effects on them would be. But their house is a happy one, and the kids seem to be thriving. The only problem is that Leo can't come to terms with the situation. He keeps muttering about taking proceedings to get the children away from Sonia and Erica, but he never actually does it. I think he knows in his heart that he couldn't provide a proper home for them like the two women can. But it does put a strain on Sonia, not knowing what Leo will do next.

Gay men, too, sometimes take custody of their children from broken marriages, but less frequently.

Some gay people, are looking at the question of fostering and adopting children. There is nothing in law which prevents this, but there is much resistance – particularly to male couples – in the agencies that arrange it. Some of these agencies actively encourage lesbian couples to apply, but others are wary of the controversy. Any gay or lesbian couple which applies to foster a child is put through the same rigorous vetting procedure as heterosexuals – in fact some have reported that they were given extra screening. Despite what is reported in some tabloid newspapers, homosexuals are given no preferential treatment. Don Smart and his partner

John Elderton, who had been fostering a young boy with Down's Syndrome, and now wanted to adopt him, wrote of their experience in *Community Care* magazine (24 January, 1991):

> The last time we tried (to adopt) we were interviewed by a psychiatrist, which at first we did not mind. I later found out that heterosexual couples would not have to undergo this interview...I contacted five London boroughs to see what response I would get from them about fostering babies with HIV and AIDS. Either they didn't have a policy about working with lesbians and gay men, or they did not see that at present there was a need for such a service. As soon as they knew I was gay they tried to ring off. Many of these places have an equal opportunities policy, but not when it comes to being gay.

There was a particularly cruel public revelation about a female couple who had succeeded in fostering a handicapped child in Newcastle. Despite their success, they were forced to give the child up when a tabloid newspaper made it into a "scandal". In many other instances, though, the couples quietly get on with the job and keep a low profile, hoping that public disclosure will not happen to them. If people are prepared to take such risks in order to foster and adopt, then it is pretty clear that they aren't doing it lightly. They have probably given a great deal of consideration to every aspect of the commitment and it will be certain that they can offer a good home and a happy environment to their charges.

Fears For The Children

The fears that attend the prospect of gay couples fostering or adopting children are often misplaced. For instance, it is assumed that if a child is fostered or adopted into a gay household, it will eventually become a homosexual itself. Research has shown, however, that children raised in those circumstances are no more likely to turn out homosexual than anyone else in the population. This fear harks back to the old idea that homosexuality is in some way "catching" or can be "learned". Most gay couples who have charge of children will have given a great deal of thought to how their child might be pressured, and most have reported that they try very hard not to push their charge one way or the other, but to allow him or her to make up their own mind in their own time. Few heterosexual parents can claim the same.

There may also be a fear that children will be taunted and teased at school because they have "two mummies" or "two daddies", but research carried out among children from same-sex households showed that this was not a significant problem in their lives. They were much more likely to suffer at the hands of their school chums because they were fat or had some other physical abnormality.

Assessing the available evidence in her book *The Marrying Kind*, Brenda Maddox wrote:

> No evidence has turned up that the children of homosexuals are more mixed-up, disturbed, or, for that matter, homosexual, than the children of divorced parents in general.

One of the first large-scale studies of the children of lesbian mothers was by Dr Martha Kirkpatrick and was published by The University of California in 1976. The twenty children in her study certainly did have problems – but they were the familiar ones associated with divorce. The children were worried that they had been the cause of their parents' marital breakdown; they were also worried that they would lose either parent later. But there was no sign of any of them becoming homosexual, sexually confused or disturbed.

Dr Pepper Schwartz, a sociologist from the University of Washington, also found after much research that there was no difference between the development of children in heterosexual and homosexual households.

Meanwhile, Dr Richard Green of the State University of New York did a psychiatric evaluation of thirty-seven children being raised by female homosexuals or by transsexual parents. In all the teenagers, sexual orientation was "developing in an appropriate pattern". Dr Green concluded that children do not get their sexual orientation from imitating, or being influenced by, their parents alone. It appears that the child takes his or her sexual model from society as a whole. A boy learns what a man is like from watching television and from his school friends as well as from his father. If he feels himself to be male, he'll pick up the signals from everywhere. Dr Green also found that teasing at school was not a major problem: the children either hadn't been teased or if they had, they'd shrugged it off. One boy had told him: "She can be anything she wants, as long as she's still my mother."

How do I react?

So, how do you cope if you have grandchildren living with your son or daughter in a gay relationship? The answer seems to be: accept and support. Not only will this benefit the children, it will also ensure that you keep your own contact with them. This is Jenny's story:

> When my daughter June took her daughter to live with another woman, I was heartbroken. I said I'd never speak to her again and that she was leaving the child open to corruption. That resulted in me distancing myself not only from June, but from my grandchild as well. It hurt like hell, and eventually I had to go round and see them both. I've now managed to overcome my fears and I recognise that they're OK and don't have many problems. I now take my grand-daughter out with me, and look after her when the girls want to go away somewhere together. It's taken a lot of adjusting to, but I don't think my grand-daughter is any the worse for it – and I'm a lot happier.

5.
AIDS

AIDS means Acquired Immunodeficiency Syndrome and its mention strikes fear into the heart of most people.

If you are the parent of a gay son, probably the first thing that sprang to your mind when you found out was: has he got AIDS? There is no doubt that AIDS has, in the developed world, hit the gay community hardest. Many thousands of young men have succumbed to the condition in Britain – hundreds of thousands in the United States. Many more are infected with HIV, the virus which can lead to the onset of AIDS. The pandemic is likely to get much worse before it gets better.

So, what will this mean for your own child? Does his gayness mean that he will inevitably die from AIDS? The simple answer to that is: no. Although a significant number of people in the gay community are infected with the virus, they still represent only a minority. Most gay people are not infected and there is no reason why they ever should be.

It may be that your son is one of those unfortunate to have been diagnosed as HIV positive. If this is the case, there is still hope.

But let's start at the beginning. Despite the fact that AIDS represents a huge threat to world health, ignorance about it persists. It is as though people deliberately avoid the facts and assiduously refuse to educate themselves. This is an attitude that can prove fatal. Knowledge about the disease, its modes of transmission and the ways of avoiding infection are the only ways we have at present of protecting ourselves against it. Although research is being directed towards it, there is no reassuring vaccination, and no cure once the virus has been contracted. Avoidance is currently our only defence.

What is AIDS?

Acquired Immunodeficiency Syndrome (AIDS) is a weakening of the body's immune system so that its natural defence mechanisms are no longer able to fight off illness. This weakening is brought about by infection with the Human Immunodeficiency Virus (HIV). The excellent handbook *AIDS: a Guide to Survival* (GMP Publishers) explains what happens after a person has become infected with HIV:

> The body then becomes vulnerable to specific types of life-threatening disease: viral, fungal, protozoal, and (occasionally) bacterial infections, as well as rare cancers. These are known as 'opportunistic' infections and cancers because they take advantage of the opportunity provided by the AIDS-damaged immune system to invade the body and rapidly multiply out of control – often with fatal consequences. Thus, strictly speaking, no-one dies from AIDS. They are actually killed by opportunistic diseases which the AIDS-impaired body is unable to resist."

Once AIDS has been diagnosed, diseases such as Kaposi's sarcoma (a skin cancer) and Pneumocystis carinii pneumonia may develop. Normally the body would fight off such rare infections as a matter of course.

HIV can enter the bloodstream in a number of ways: through sexual activity (and some homosexual activities seem to be particularly efficient at transmitting the virus); through injecting with a hypodermic needle which has already been used by someone infected, and has still has traces of their blood; by transfusion of infected blood (although in developed countries, this mode of transmission has been eliminated by screening and heat treatment); and by use of blood products by haemophiliacs (this, too, has been eliminated, although not before many haemophiliacs had been affected).

Although HIV can be passed from men to women (and vice versa) through ordinary vaginal sex, it happens less frequently – at least in the developed world – than when two men have anal sex. Consequently the AIDS epidemic was first apparent in the developed world in the gay community of America. In the third world, particularly in Africa, the disease is taking a different course and affecting mainly heterosexuals. Added factors such as poverty, poor resistance to disease and the routine re-use of hypodermic needles. AIDS is wreaking havoc in some African countries, destroying vast numbers of young, productive men and women and their families.

But what about your son? (Lesbians are one of the lowest risk groups for AIDS, and the syndrome is almost unknown among gay women, so we will concentrate on gay men). What does this mean for him?

If, like most gay men, he is at present free of infection, there are several things he can do to ensure he stays that way. First, and most important, by the adoption of safer sex practices. I recognise that at this point many parents will be cringing, not wanting to recognise that their sons have sex with other men, let alone that they should be modifying it for safety's sake. But we are talking about survival, and if you wish your son to remain healthy and free of this dreadful affliction, then it is important that you know how he can manage it.

Safer sex means not allowing the bodily fluids of other people to get inside your own body. "Bodily fluids" means blood, semen, urine and faeces. Although some traces of HIV have been detected in saliva, it is thought that these are too minute to be of consequence. One of the best ways of preventing semen passing from one person into another during sexual intercourse is for the active partner to wear a condom.

If you want to ensure that your gay son knows about safer sex, ask him to read about it. You could get him some literature from one of the gay book shops listed at the back of the book. There are several titles which explain, in clear, common-sense language, what safer sex is and how it's practised. Any of the AIDS education organisations, such as the Terrence Higgins Trust, will also be able to provide relevant material. This is particularly important for younger gay men who maybe ignorant or irresponsible.

It's probably difficult for you to imagine that you'll be able to talk to your son about his intimate sex life, but in these circumstances it might be advisable to check out that he is well-informed. When life and death are the issue, it's time to put propriety to one side.

Perhaps you could broach the subject first of all in a general kind of way: "AIDS is a very worrying thing, you read so much about it. Are you doing anything to protect yourself against it?" If he reacts with embarrassment, or tries to change the subject, be persistent, and let him know that you aren't being critical or judgmental. If there is any sign that you are disapproving of his lifestyle, you'll see him close up like a clam, and then it will be even more difficult to make sure that he has the right kind of lifesaving information.

If you really can't say it to him directly, why not just get the information and discreetly leave it where he can find it and read it? You might also enclose a packet of condoms.

Being open and caring is the best way to set up lines of communication between you, but if there is no tradition in your family of discussing these personal issues, then it might be difficult to be direct. Here is Mary, talking about her son, Jeremy, and her inability to get beyond the 'blush barrier' when talking to him:

> I was worried sick about Jerry and all this AIDS business, it seemed to be on the television every night and in the papers all the time. But I didn't know how to raise the issue with him. We've never been very open in our family about our feelings, and especially not about sex. It's always been a subject we've avoided, and my husband actually forbids the children to mention it. It's unfair to project our hang-ups on to them, I know, but it's hard to change after all these years. I skirted round it a few times, but never got to asking him any questions. I wanted to know whether he thought he had it or how he could avoid getting it. But I never did ask him, and I still worry because I don't know what's going on in his life. I suppose we have ourselves to blame for never being open about sex.

If your son is involved in the gay community, it is likely that he has already come across safer sex advice, but that doesn't mean that he is abiding by it. There is evidence that an increasing number of younger people are disregarding these safety-first principles and laying themselves open to infection. Why do they do it, you might ask? Why don't they just give up sex and be safe? The answer is, of course, that the sexual urge is very strong in human beings – stronger often than the fear of disease. The sexual impulse can cause normally sane and rational people to risk their marriages, their families, their reputations. Couple this with the feeling of immortality which is so strong among young people, and you have a recipe for disaster. Young people literally think that it can't happen to them, that they are somehow safe. It can lead them into taking unnecessary risks.

There is no easy answer but to try and keep the message of safer sex fresh and current. If you can't discuss it, make sure he has supportive literature. Ensure that he has the gay press to read: this often has the latest information on developments in AIDS and will keep the subject to the forefront of your son's mind. Research by the advertising industry has shown that people are more likely to trust and believe information when it comes from their own community than when it comes from 'official' sources. That is why the gay press is so important in getting the safer sex message over and keeping it a live issue. Why not treat your son to a subscription to one of the other journals published for gay readers?

Naturally your son may be suspicious of your efforts to encourage him to be responsible in his personal relationships. He may feel that your constant harping on AIDS is a subtle way of expressing your disapproval of his way of life. If he suspects that is your motive – and ask yourself frequently whether it is – then he will probably disregard what you say and avoid listening to you.

At this stage you may well be uncomfortable with the thought of your child having a sex life. This is understandable and, depending on his age and psychological maturity, you may feel it is reasonable to intervene. But be fair in your assessment, there is a difference between trying to restrict a fifteen-year-old and trying the same thing on a twenty-year-old. There comes a time when you have to recognise that your child has a right to his own body and, despite your discomfort and unease, you will have to respect that.

However hard you try and whatever precautions you take, it is unlikely that you will be able to stop your children – straight or gay – from eventually expressing their sexuality. Your choice, then, is to be realistic and try to ensure that your son is as safe as possible, or to keep on resisting and possibly fostering an irresponsible and rebellious attitude. Your son may actually choose to behave dangerously just to defy you!

These are difficult choices made necessary by the nature of the enemy – a brutal, relentless killer that is stalking our gay sons.

Remember, knowledge and a sensible approach to sex are the only protection.

Let's look at some questions parents ask about this subject.

But why would he have sex with someone with AIDS. Surely you can tell they're ill?

When someone is infected with HIV they can remain perfectly healthy for many years – maybe even indefinitely. Some people have been HIV positive for more than ten years and have not developed AIDS. But they still remain capable of passing on the virus to other people. There is no way that appearance alone can tell you whether a person is HIV positive. (It is important to understand the difference between being simply HIV positive and having "full-blown" AIDS. Infection with HIV, as we've said, does not necessarily mean that a person is ill. You can have HIV in your body for many years and remain totally free of any symptoms. Only when the virus wins its constant battle with the body's immune system does the sufferer become ill, falling prey to what are called "opportunistic infections". It is at this point that AIDS is diagnosed. One illness follows another, gradually wearing the sufferer down.)

Should he have a test?

The implications of taking an HIV antibody test are so potentially serious that it really does have to be the choice of the person concerned. Such is the prejudice that surrounds AIDS that if it becomes known that an individual has even taken the test – whether the result is positive or negative – that person can lose their job, their home, and their friends. Insurance companies may refuse cover, a mortgage may be difficult to obtain and other petty discriminations may follow. The British Government has recently introduced legislation which does give some protection, but it has yet to be tested for effectiveness.

However, there is a move towards encouraging people to take the test. Discovering that you are HIV positive sooner, rather than later, can improve your prospects of surviving longer. New treatments for people who are HIV positive are being developed all the time, and these can significantly slow down the progression to AIDS. The longer you can fight off AIDS, the better the chances that some other more predictable, less dangerous treatments will be developed in the meantime.

But no-one should take the test without being counselled beforehand – and afterwards if the result is positive. All the relevant information should be made available in order that the person can make an informed decision about whether to proceed with the test, there are psychological as well as practical considerations: will the person be able to cope with the news if the test proves positive? What effect will it have on the family? Will he find the support he needs?

How can I help if he's HIV positive?

If your son chooses to share the news with you that he has tested positive for HIV, hopefully you'll do your best to support him. If he tells you soon after he has found out himself, he may need your reassurance that you'll stand by him. It's likely that he'll be depressed, confused and frightened for a considerable time. Even though he may have suspected that he would test positive, the shock can still be devastating when the news is actually confirmed.

Most gay men who have taken the test and found themselves to be HIV positive, have begun to explore ways of preventing or delaying the onset of the full syndrome. In most cases, the reason people took the test was so that they could begin appropriate therapies which might help them remain healthy longer.

There are many different approaches, and your son may well be looking at these. In the AIDS community there is a strong belief that people with HIV are not "victims" and should not regard themselves as such. A victim is helpless, but people with HIV and AIDS are not – they can take many steps to help themselves, this is called "self-empowerment" or taking charge of your own life. As well as new drugs which are being developed to boost the immune system, the person who is HIV positive can change their lifestyle to become generally stronger and healthier and therefore less likely to become ill quickly. Many gay men are on fitness regimes which include a new diet, exercise, meditation, relaxation and a range of alternative therapies such as homeopathy, acupuncture, aroma therapy, massage and so on.

Naturally with an illness like this, charlatans are also in operation, offering "cures" and quack remedies. Be wary of anyone who tries to sell you unproved medicines or treatments – they are liable to be very expensive and lead to bitter disappointment.

The importance of confidentiality

You must also respect your son's privacy. If he has told you, but asked you not to tell anyone else – or only selected other people – then please try to keep it that way. It may be that you are worried and need to share the burden with someone else, but the consequences of telling the wrong person at the wrong time can be disastrous. The myths and fears surrounding AIDS are still very potent, and reactions can't be predicted, even from those you consider will be most understanding.

Lifestyle and stress

Naturally, if you can conquer your fears about your son's lifestyle and come to terms with it, it will take a great burden from his shoulders. It is recognised by those who work with AIDS that stress is a major risk factor in the development of the disease. You can take some of the stress out of your son's life by being non-judgmental about his friends, his life and his sexual orientation.

Many gay men who are living with HIV or AIDS refuse to allow the disease to dominate their lives:

> I suspected that I might be HIV positive, but I didn't take the test, and tried to convince myself that everything would be OK. I had actually come to believe that it couldn't happen to me, that I was somehow special or lucky. I suppose it's a way for the mind to cope with the worry. Then I got a bout of pneumonia, which took me to hospital, and they told me then that I had developed AIDS. They got me over that crisis, and when I was up and about again, I decided that I'd find out as much as I could about the disease and fight it with all my might. I'm not ready to die yet, I'm only twenty-eight. I found out that it was important to have a positive outlook and not become fatalistic about it. I got a lot of support from an AIDS group who showed me the things I could do to help myself and make myself stronger and fitter. I felt good about taking all these steps to help myself. I always went along with treatments that were offered, but I

did as much as I could for myself, too. When I felt that I had a chance of surviving, I decided to tell my parents. They were upset, but when they saw that I looked and felt fitter than I have done for some time, they calmed down. I suppose they thought I was wrong or that there'd been a mistake. I couldn't convince them that it wasn't a soap opera, and there hadn't been a mistake at the hospital where they'd got my notes mixed up with someone else's.

It's been great that my parents have been so good about it, but I must say that my father's constant harping on health gets on my nerves a bit. Whenever he rings me he always starts out with tentative little questions like: 'Is everything OK? How are you feeling? Are you keeping well?' I have to tell him that I'm perfectly all right, and we've made a pact that if there are any developments in my health, I will tell them about it. I won't lie to them or cover things up. But while I'm well, I don't want to be regarded as an invalid. I'm living life to the full – I've still got my job, which I hold down well, and I still have a social life. I don't want to spend the rest of my life preparing for death. I want to live while I'm alive, I'll be dead for long enough. So, it isn't time for me to be making my fond farewells yet, and I'm hoping it won't be for a long time. That's why I insist on being called a person living with AIDS rather than a person dying from AIDS. After all, it's quite likely that you or I will die in a motor accident if we drive a lot, so AIDS is only one life-threatening risk I'm living with.

AIDS in the family

For many families, AIDS is a reality. They have discovered that not only is their son gay, he also has AIDS. This double blow can precipitate a crisis that can be shattering for all concerned. Not only are all the previously mentioned doubts, fears and anger about homosexuality experienced, there is the extra burden of terminal illness.

It is when the revelation has been made that the recriminations set in. Listen to Anne, whose thirty-two year old son Nigel returned from his home in London two years ago to tell them that he is gay and has AIDS.

It was a total shock to us, we were all dumb struck when he told us. We'd no idea that he was homosexual and had always assumed that he had girlfriends in London. Then we discovered that he had been living a life that we just never imagined. I was angry at him, and furious with his boyfriend, Jim. I spoke to Jim on the phone and accused him of being the cause of my son having AIDS. 'If it hadn't been for you this would never have happened,' I said. It was stupid really, because I'd never met the man, and I had no idea what kind of life they lived together. I didn't know whether Jim had AIDS, too and, as it turned out, neither did he. He was as worried as I was. Eventually he had a test which proved negative, so it couldn't have been him that gave my Nigel the disease. But I'm afraid at the beginning I wasn't thinking logically.

Not only were we trying to come to terms with this new idea of who Nigel was, we were also trying to think of what was going to happen to him as the disease progressed. Although we'd been told often enough that we weren't in any danger of catching it, there was always this niggling worry, and I did silly things like making Nigel use his own crockery and cutlery and towels. It was cruel of me, I realise that now, but at the time I didn't know any better. We were all so sorry for him, and we didn't want to do anything that would make his life even worse. His brothers and sisters, who are all living away from home, were marvellous. They've always been very close and they wanted to do anything they could to support him. I just had to get myself educated so that I could cope. Nigel wanted to go back to his home in London and let Jim look after him, I wanted him to stay here in Leicester with us, so that we could help him. In the end he went back to London, and I started to go and stay with him for weeks at a stretch. As he got more and more ill I stayed longer and longer. There were big problems between me and Jim about who should do what. I suppose in a way I was taking over, but I could be around all day whereas Jim had to go off to work.

I was impressed by the way Nigel's friends rallied round, and at the level of care he got from various agencies. It changed my whole idea about what gay people are and also about AIDS. Jim and I worked through Nigel's illness together and we found out a lot about ourselves in the process. I've got a totally different attitude about a lot of things after going through this experience. Nigel died peacefully in his sleep at home where he wanted to be. We knew that it was time for him to go, and we asked the rest of the family to come down to be with him, which they all did.

Does it sound callous to say that AIDS did something wonderful for our family? I will always remember Nigel's bravery during those last few months and Jim's loyalty and the love of all the people who helped us. If you'd told me that this is how I would feel at the beginning, I wouldn't have believed you.

The first thing to remember is that HIV cannot be contracted through ordinary social contact. You cannot get AIDS by shaking hands with someone, kissing them on the cheek, by sharing their crockery and cutlery or from a lavatory seat. You cannot get AIDS from hugging someone or stroking their hair. You cannot get AIDS from breathing the same air as someone – even if they are coughing and sneezing. If you have someone with AIDS living in your house, then you are in no danger from them as far as normal day-to-day living is concerned. On the contrary, they are in greater danger from you: if their immune system is compromised, they are much more likely to get dangerous infections from you than you are from them. Infections which are minor to you can become grave illnesses for people with AIDS.

Ordinary hygiene precautions will ensure that the danger is eliminated. If there is any spilled blood or other bodily fluid – urine, faeces, semen or vomit – then this can be cleared up quite effectively using ordinary household bleach or strong detergent. Rubber gloves need only be worn when this kind of cleaning up is to be done. Laundry doesn't need special attention, except if it is badly soiled by bodily fluids, when it should be boiled. Remember, the virus is relatively fragile once it is outside the body, and dies quickly after being exposed to the air. There is no need to worry that it might somehow "linger" on door handles or handkerchiefs or towels. On this subject, the psychotherapist Don Clark has written:

Anyone who has chosen to work as a person who helps other people has had the experience of failing to help at some time because of fear. Fear makes failure more likely. More often than not, it is the person or people we are trying to help who help us to overcome our fears. We fear that which is unknown or unfamiliar. I recently spoke with a physician who is not gay who said, 'It was difficult for me to have to admit that when AIDS patients began to be admitted to the hospital, I was afraid to deal with them or walk into their rooms, not because I was afraid of the disease, but because I was afraid of them.' She told me several stories of patients who were so kind and understanding. 'They knew the trouble I was having before I knew. They were my teachers. They even helped me through my shame when I did realise what had been going on.'

How the family copes with AIDS

The crisis which AIDS creates in the family has been examined by several researchers, and has been shown to follow an identifiable pattern in most cases. The phases have been described by Nancy C. Lovejoy in the book *Homosexuality and Family Relations* (eds Bozett and Sussman, Harrington Park Press, 1990). The first phase was labelled "Crisis" and is characterised by:

1. Shock: This includes lack of emotion, apathy, withdrawal and physical symptoms such as heart palpitations and breathlessness. When family members are experiencing shock they may become highly emotional, crying and speaking hysterically. They will be unable to make complex decisions. Some families immediately reject their AIDS-affected child and push him out of the family structure, others rush to help. Older parents, it seems, have more positive responses than their younger counterparts, and those of a more liberal leaning will react better than those who are traditionally conservative in their outlook.

Other aspects of shock might refer to the workings of the health care system. Some families have not had to negotiate the complicated and bureaucratic system before and become shocked at its shortcomings. Others were shocked at the attitudes of some health workers, who seemed homophobic and ill-informed about AIDS. This is likely to occur most frequently outside the large cities, where the incidence of AIDS is still relatively low. There may also be shocks in store for families as they come up against the social injustices which are meted out routinely to homosexuals and to those suffering from AIDS-related illnesses: evictions, firings, rejections and dismissals. Those families who come to the AIDS-affected person later in the illness may be appalled by changes in his physical appearance. The realisation that the condition is irreversible also deeply shocks families.

It's important for families in shock from discovering they have a son with AIDS to get as much support as they can. They should make sure they are well-informed, and have access to a crisis counselling line. Family members should be watched for signs of depression, anxiety and even suicidal impulses.

2. Denial: When they first hear the news, family members might temporarily deny that it is true. They may suffer anger, depression and talk about the illness in an impersonal way, as though it is someone else's problem. This denial is usually selective – that is, they'll acknowledge that their child is ill, but deny some aspects of the illness such as what is causing it and that it is likely to be terminal. In some ways this denial is a way for families to cope with their day-to-day lives. If they can put off the truth for as long as possible, life doesn't have to be too badly disrupted.

As a result of this denial, those who are caring for the person with AIDS may not be taking the right measures to protect their own health and that of the sufferer. Most experienced workers in the AIDS field recognise this and try to help families come to terms with the full implications of what is happening to them.

3. Anxiety: Families who have a gay son are often concerned about AIDS; this becomes a severe anxiety if he has been diagnosed as HIV positive. I've already suggested the practical steps you can take if he is HIV positive, but the nagging anxiety might become disproportionate causing all kinds of other symptoms, such as depression, compulsive information-seeking, over-dependence on other people, withdrawal from others, insomnia and disorientation. The only way to tackle that anxiety is to ensure that you are properly informed about AIDS and the available treatments. Find a sympathetic person who will give you the information you need. If you, or anyone in your family, feel that the anxiety about this issue is getting out of proportion, then you should seek help. It won't help you or your son, who needs your support, if you become ill through constant worry and misunderstanding.

Phase Two is called "Transition" and its manifestations include:

1. Fear/AIDS Hysteria: Because of the sensationalised reporting of AIDS in the media in the early days of the epidemic, many family members are frightened that they themselves may be at risk of becoming infected. These fears are compounded by other worries, such as whether the family will be scorned by its friends and neighbours. Naturally, family members are also afraid of losing their loved one. Fear of bereavement affects people in different ways – some parents may withhold their affection from their AIDS-affected son, others may keep vigils, especially during stays in hospital.

One of the most successful methods of cutting through these fears is to meet someone else who has already coped with AIDS, and benefit from their experiences. If you can locate such a person – or family – and talk to them, you will find it of immense help. Perhaps one of the AIDS organisations could bring you together with other people who have already been through this terrible time.

2. Anger: People become angry about several things: about the failings of the health care system, about the fact that their child is gay (see previous chapter for further exploration of this) and sometimes at their son's partner, with whom they may not have developed a good relationship. There may be bitter arguments about funeral arrangements, financial settlements and disposal of possessions. The anger may be directed at hospital staff and volunteers who are trying to help. There may be outbursts of anger or sarcastic comments, much fault-finding, withdrawal and moody silences.

The only way to tackle this anger is to recognise its source and try to keep it under control. Once you have accepted it as a natural reaction to a crisis, you may all be able to be a little more tolerant of each other. Sometimes anger is justified and in those circumstances it is better expressed openly than internalised.

3. Depression: Depression may occur for a number of reasons, perhaps because so much anger has been turned inward. It might also be provoked by lack of support, loss of financial security and the inability to cope with all the many and varied demands that are placed on you at a time like this. Also, as the disease develops and symptoms begin to show themselves, depression can become a serious problem.

If depression is becoming a serious factor in your experience, you might consider finding some kind of professional support and counselling. Once again it is important to try and find other people who have already been through this experience and who can show you a positive role model. Your doctor may be able to help you over the immediate crisis by prescribing something to counteract your depression.

4. Guilt: Parents may feel guilty about their part in this illness. They may still be trying to come to terms with their son's homosexuality, and be asking 'Where did we go wrong? How could we have produced a son who has ended up like this?' This is made worse by the disapproval that they see all around them, and now they have the double burden of homosexuality and AIDS in the family. We have already explored the question of guilt and 'causes' of homosexuality in Chapter Two. I hope that this will have helped a little to put your mind at rest.

5. Social Support: By supporting your child through what may be his final illness you can help him, and yourself, to find new ways of looking at the world. Once you have overcome your fears and guilt about homosexuality and AIDS, you can both come to recognise that you are good people, displaying courage, commitment and concern for others. You will come to realise that it is the quality of life that matters and not the quantity. If your son is in a relationship, you may find that it is under severe strain as a result of his diagnosis. Research has shown that anxiety levels in people with AIDS are significantly lower if they have a partner who supports them through their illness. Your son's partner may well be suffering a crisis of his own, worried that he may be infected, too, and afraid of what life will be like without the support that his relationship with your son gave him. Whether you approve of the relationship or not, it will be a central focus for both their lives and the prospect of losing it will be devastating.

You may be struggling with your feelings about homosexuality, and this may be standing in your way of developing a warm and co-operative relationship with your son's partner. Please read again Chapter Four about accepting your son's friends on their own terms. You will find that it will benefit him immensely if there is minimal conflict between the most important people in his life. In return you will find you have their support and help in ministering to your son's needs. If, like Anne, you are spending time in an unfamiliar city, make sure you get all the help that is available. Keep in touch with AIDS organisations and take full advantage of what they have to offer. You will find them invaluable.

6. Information-seeking: Once the initial crisis is passed, parents who have decided to help their son to the best of their ability, will want information. There is plenty of it about. The literature about every aspect of AIDS is now substantial, so you should make best use of it to correct any misunderstandings or misinformation you might have. And because things are changing so quickly, make sure that you have up-to-date information. Once again, an AIDS organisation can be most useful here, as they have experts and counsellors on just about every topic which might arise: state benefits, latest treatments, alternative therapies and so on.

7. Altered Roles: Those involved in caring for the person with AIDS may find that they are at a loss to understand their role. If parents have not come to terms with their son's lover or friends, there may be conflicts about who should do what. This can cause the sufferer to be given a 'loyalty choice' – who is the right person to do the caring? Some parents, when they are involved in the care of their sick son, will try to pretend that everything is normal and that the son will recover from his illness or that some miracle cure will be found before it is too late. This kind of pretence is very difficult to sustain and stands in the way of the AIDS sufferer coming to terms with the truth. No preparations can be made for death while the pretence that it is not imminent continues.

Sometimes family members become so absorbed in the care of their sick child that they begin to neglect everything else – including themselves. As the son's health gradually deteriorates the care-givers are at risk of developing burn-out and consequently a sense of failure.

It may be painful for some parents to accept that their child should want a partner ('a stranger to the family' as one mother put it), to take charge of their care. Often the son will want his partner to take care of his business matters – wills, disposal or assets and so on – which can cause parents to feel resentful or slighted. However, these choices must be your son's own, and it is important that you respect them. Try not to place too many loyalty choices on your child. By agreeing in a civilised manner who will do what, it will be possible for everyone to play an important part in the care of the sick person, without adding extra strains.

If respite services are offered, don't dismiss them out of hand. Occasionally it does you good to get away from the sick room, however involved you have become in the care of your son. You should make a strong effort to ensure that there are other things happening in your life besides taking care of a sick person. It may seem selfish to you, but in the end it will benefit both of you if you can have frequent 'breathers.'

8. Hope: Hope is an important aspect of mental health. But, you might ask, what hope is there with AIDS? Surely a terminal illness is the very definition of hopelessness? This depends of what you are expecting. With new treatments and self-help plans it is possible to help a person with AIDS to live a much longer and more productive life than before. There is always hope that something even more effective will come along – after all, research in this field is intense. Strangely, studies of those families dealing with AIDS, have shown that they often develop a new sense of hope for the future despite the fact that their child has died. They have a new image of themselves, made good by their efforts, their altruism and the proof that they had strengths which they never before realised.

It is important to set goals for yourself which will take you, perhaps, five years into the future. They should be concrete, realistic goals. If you have something to aim for, you will not become hopeless. If you cannot do this on your own, then perhaps a counsellor specialising in working with families affected by AIDS might be able to help you.

The fourth phase is "Anticipatory Mourning and Bereavement". Anticipatory mourning begins when it becomes increasingly clear that the patient is in the final stages of illness. At this stage those caring for him will help him complete any unfinished business, will assure him that his wishes will be respected after he is dead, and they will often give him permission to let go of life. There are many touching stories of mothers and fathers who have cared for their son through his decline and when they feel the suffering has gone on too long, they have encouraged their child to "let go."

Some mothers have expressed that this was their ultimate act of love: to encourage their child gently out of a life that has become too painful for any of them to endure.

Bereavement: The loss of a child is a traumatic event for any parent, but if that loss is caused by AIDS, there are extra problems. Parents may feel guilt as well as sadness, depression, and loss. It is normal for the bereavement process to continue for many months, even years, and there is nothing that can be done to shorten it. However, it is important that you talk about your loss. You may feel like isolating yourself at first, but this should not be allowed to go on for too long, and you should seek support and maybe even counselling. There are some excellent books about coping with bereavement, and you might find these helpful. However bad it seems at the start, please try to remember that one day the pain will diminish, and although you'll never be able to forget entirely, there will be other things in life. The experience, in the end, will have enriched you and made you a person who can be proud.

Some parents were able to take care of their child for many months at home, but the final illness is often endured in hospital. The attitudes of health staff will vary according to the part of the country and the establishment, but certainly in hospitals which are familiar with the treatment of AIDS-related complaints (mainly in big cities) there is less likelihood of homophobia or AIDS hysteria adding to the distress.

Your son, and perhaps his partner or friends, will benefit immensely from your support and understanding, and you will benefit from theirs. It is extremely important that you try to break down any barriers which may arise between you. Read again the preceding chapters, and try to make sense of them in your own circumstances.

AIDS is an enormous tragedy. It is affecting different parts of the world in different ways. Wherever it appears its effects are devastating, not only for those who are struck down, but also for those who care for them. The hystcrical myths which still cling to it in the Western world are bound up with the inability to accept homosexuality. As the tragedy escalates, some of these myths are being dismantled, although they die hard. Tens of thousands of families have had to face this horror, and many have done so with formidable courage and resourcefulness. Others have been unable to cope and have walked away from their gay son, leaving him to die isolated from his roots.

Those who have taken their courage in both hands and squarely faced up to AIDS have often said they were enriched by the experience. They have lost a son, but through that tragedy they have gained a new insight into themselves and their lives. Wherever you go within the community that cares for people living with AIDS, you will find compassion on a staggering scale.

To end this chapter, here is what one mother wrote after the death of her son from AIDS:

It is two years since Derek died and although much of the acute pain has disappeared, and I now sleep at night, I do not let a day go by without thinking about him. He died relatively quickly after he became ill, only two short months, but so much was achieved in that time. I grew so much closer to him and we talked in a way that we had never talked before. I think I always knew that he was gay, even though he never formally told me. As he lay in bed I would sit beside him, hour after hour, just looking at his face, his dear lovely face, and realise how much I loved him and how apart we'd been. When he was conscious and his mind was working properly, we would talk about old times, and I brought some of our old photo albums to the hospital so we could go through our lives together. It was during those little reminiscence sessions that I came to realise that I'd lost him emotionally when he was about fifteen. I suppose it must have been about that time that he began to realise that he was gay. He was always a gentle child and never played violent games with other boys. He much preferred more sensitive pastimes. But he couldn't share his feelings with me then, and I didn't ask him to. So he went through all his adolescence wrapped up in this sense of failure and differentness. And I hadn't helped him at all. I feel so guilty about that, but it's too late now.

He left home when he was eighteen and went to live in Manchester. He said it was for a job he wanted at the TV station, but I knew there were other reasons. He didn't find the stimulation he needed at home, and I could see that he was lonely. We were sorry to see him go, and once he was away we grew even more apart. He'd come home perhaps three times a year, most Christmases, but he always seemed uncomfortable and anxious to get back to his friends in Manchester.

It was on one of his Christmas visits that I noticed how pale and thin he looked. I asked if he was OK. He broke down in tears and told his father and me that he had AIDS. We said that we'd stand by him, and look after him. He decided that he was going to leave his job and move back with us. I was relieved about that, because I knew that I'd be able to look after him best here in our own house. As I said, it wasn't a long illness and eventually he went into hospital for the last few days. He was unconscious for the whole of the time and then he just slipped away at three o'clock one morning. We weren't there when he died, they just told us about it the following morning.

I was devastated, there was so much sorting out to do, so many things that I hadn't been able to work out with him. Now it was too late and he was gone. But I'd managed to make all the arrangements as he wanted them, a secular funeral and all his friends invited. They all came round here afterwards for a meal, and I was proud to be among them. They were a great bunch of young people and I was glad that they had been my son's friends.

Since then I've read a lot about AIDS, and found out all the things parents need to know before it happens. I've decided that I'm going to devote a lot of my time to helping other people who might be going through what I went through. I work on an AIDS helpline, which has made me aware of how much fear there is around. People ring up sick with worry, and I'm glad to be able to help in some way.

I'm determined that my son's death is not going to be meaningless. I'm going to ensure that through our experience together, I'm going to help other people in the same situation. I feel strong enough to do that now, whereas before all this, I'd have thought it was beyond me. It's important work, and I'm proud to be involved.

6.
The gay community

As you talk to your child about his or her life, you will eventually hear mention of the 'gay community'. Your son or daughter will probably already feel part of this community or, if not, will be hoping to become part of it. He or she may see it as possibly providing a salvation from loneliness and isolation; it is the place where they may find friends and even a partner, it's where they can relax and be themselves.

But where is this community? Why can't it be pinpointed? Many parents fear that their sons or daughters are entering some kind of secret society, or a ghetto which will restrict and imprison them.

The gay community actually exists wherever gay people get together, it is constituted of people rather than places (although places are important as landmarks). For instance, gay people will feel they are socialising in the 'gay community' if they are invited to a party which is to be attended by other gay people. It's an attitude of mind as much as a series of locations. The historian and sociologist Jeffrey Weeks put it this way:

> The lesbian and gay community rarely exists as a geographical entity; it does not necessarily involve any common ideological, economic, political or social features; it exists more in the mind than on the ground. It is nevertheless a reality, for it is based around the idea of positive lesbian and gay identities that have been forged against so many odds during these past decades.

This community is beginning to feel much more solid and established to those involved. It even has its own symbols, recognisable to everyone who feels they are part of the gay

community. One such is the pink triangle, which will be prominent
at most gay events. It represents the mark used by the nazis in their
concentration camps to identify homosexuals. Jews were assigned a
yellow star, whilst homosexuals wore the pink triangle. Nowadays
it is worn as a badge of honour by gay people all over the world.
Another common symbol is the Freedom Flag or Rainbow Flag,
which was created to represent through colour all the positive
elements of being gay.

In most large towns in this country there are now pubs and
clubs which have exclusively gay and lesbian customers. There is
also a vast network of local groups set up by gay people themselves
to provide social outlets where no commercial facility exists. There
are shops run by and for gay people, holiday companies which
cater exclusively for gay clients, gay newspapers and magazines,
counselling and befriending services for those who are lonely and
unhappy, there are groups dealing with the problems of AIDS,
support agencies for the parents of lesbians and gay men and
organisations given over to political campaigning. Indeed, the gay
community now has a well-established infrastructure.

But often it is misrepresented. You may have read some
newspaper commentators denying that the gay community exists at
all. How can there be a community, argue these journalists, for
people who have nothing in common but their sexual appetites?
Why should such a diverse and random selection of individuals
want to be lumped together? After all, in "real" communities (they
usually cite the Jewish community or the West Indian community),
families and neighbours support each other, they are connected not
only culturally but also by living in the same area or
neighbourhood. Their whole lives share a common bond. Such a
claim could not be made for homosexuals, who come from every
race, religion, class, culture, age group and geographical location.
What is the common thread that weaves through the lives of such a
divergent cross section of the population?

The obvious answer is that they share a sexual preference, and
yet even the most widely differing members of the gay community
share more than that. For instance, a gay male company director
might not at first sight seem to have much in common with a
lesbian woman, living in a council flat with her two children from
a previous marriage. But, in fact, they do share some common
interests – even though they, themselves, may not recognise them.
For instance, they both live with the possibility that at some stage

in their life they may suffer discrimination because of their sexuality. Although the company director may be secure financially at present, he might just as easily fall foul of a homophobic managing director as the lesbian woman might to an anti-gay judge who takes her children away from her. Both will share the same need for love and companionship and, if they have come to terms with their sexuality, they will probably find their way, at some stage, in to the gay community to try and satisfy that need for friends or a more permanent partner. Their paths may never cross and, even if they do, they may not get on together, but they are both honorary members of the gay community whether they like it or not.

So, let's look more closely at some of the many strands that make up this huge, loosely-knit subculture.

Clubs And Pubs

Pubs and night-clubs which cater exclusively for gay men and lesbians play an important part in the gay community. These commercial operations are often referred to collectively as the "gay scene". Often such establishments are portrayed in newspapers as sinister and sordid (indeed, it's unlikely that a gay pub could be mentioned in a tabloid news report without the addition of a judgmental adjective), but are they really as dreadful as they're painted?

The less desirable elements in society have traditionally gathered at public houses. We've all heard about pubs with reputations for drug pushing, or where stolen goods change hands, or prostitutes gather, or where violence is a regular occurrence. Some of these pubs deserve their reputations, but it is unfair to lump gay pubs in with these dens of antisocial behaviour just because they are gay pubs. Nowadays gay pubs are legal and are granted licences like any other establishment. They have emerged from the "twilight world" of semi-legality into the brightly-lit world of commercial enterprise. Gay pubs are big business, and are often operated by large breweries with reputations to consider. The days when gay pubs were forced to skirt around the law are over, although the reputation lingers on.

There are doubtless some gay pubs which wouldn't be to everyone's taste, but that is true across the board. Mostly gay pubs are just places where gay men and women can relax, be themselves and socialise in an accepting environment. Of course, for some homophobic people, that is reason enough to regard them as undesirable, but it is hard on the people who use them.

Here is how one older gay man sees gay bars, as recounted in the book *Gay and Gray* (Berger: Alyson, Publications, 1982):

> There is a certain comradeship in a gay bar. Everywhere else you go you are sort of 'in hiding' because you assume everyone else is heterosexual. In a gay bar the tables are turned: everyone is assumed to be gay. This becomes very apparent when some straight people walk in by accident and gradually discover that they're in the wrong place. They feel uncomfortable, just like we might in a straight bar. It's really quite amusing. It is also true that, in the bar my friend likes, the same people are there week after week. So it becomes like the neighbourhood tavern: a place to meet your friends.

Some gay pubs are quiet, subdued and welcoming; others are loud, rackety with a strong element of sexual competition. This fits the pattern of pubs generally, whether patronised by gay or straight people. The major difference is that often specialist pubs are the only place where gay people can gather to meet each other in relative safety. Unlike heterosexuals, gay people do not find endless opportunities to socialise together. In a large town there may be one or, if they're lucky, two gay pubs to choose from, whereas straight people might be able to choose from thirty or forty. But, as gay pubs proliferate, they need to compete to attract customers, and so the standard goes up accordingly. *Gay Times* (June, 1991) said of gay bars in the 90s:

> In recent years licensing restrictions have eased to allow pubs and bars to adopt a more Continental approach to the selling of alcohol and food where the distinction between restaurants, cafes and pubs become blurred. Pubs are no longer the preserve of drinkers hidden behind frosted glass or closed curtains. Cafes are no longer places where you can only drink apple juice or take tea over a seersucker tablecloth.

Gay pubs and bars, therefore, are no longer the seedy dives of popular imagination (although some deliberately go for this effect).

Their young customers demand high standards, the licensing authorities demand exemplary behaviour and everyone is happy.

The gay pub often becomes the primary focus of gay life in a town. It is here that gay people can meet each other, make friends, chat about their lives, find out about other events which might be on offer (some pubs have a 'community' notice board which might bring news of coach trips, parties, discos, accommodation or work opportunities, social groups and so on). It is at the pub that copies of gay newspapers might be available.

Sometimes pubs and clubs are described as "mixed" which means that they are frequented by both heterosexual and homosexual customers. This is becoming more and more usual as the barriers between young gay people and their straight friends begin to break down. Sometimes "mixed" also means that both gay men and lesbians use it. In small towns where the gay population is insufficient to support more than one pub, this is quite frequent, but sometimes (especially in London and other big cities) the pubs have almost totally male clientele. This happens for a number of reasons, one of which is that lesbian women often feel unwelcome in pubs where they are in a small minority, and so would prefer to find their own space. Lesbian separatism is quite pronounced on the social scene, women feel they have different priorities to men and also have less money to spend, and so prefer to find places to be together where they are not pushed into a corner and marginalised. Pubs, clubs and discos catering exclusively for lesbians are few and far between, but where they do exist, they are generally popular. One such venue was described in an article by Sandra Barwick which appeared in *The Independent* newspaper (6 July, 1991). The club is called Venus Rising and is situated Brixton, London.

> Venus Rising is claimed to be the biggest event of its kind in Europe. The monthly event attracts an average of 900 gay women, who were this week seething and gyrating on the huge dance floor...The atmosphere was entirely relaxed and unthreatening. The security women on the door said that apart from the odd fight between girlfriends, the only scuffles came at the end of the night when women sometimes refused to go home!...Certainly if Venus Rising is anything to go by, these days the well of loneliness is a pretty crowded place to be.

Gay night-clubs are like most others: they are places where people drink, dance and look for romance. Once again they might become the focus for illegal activity (such as drug pushing), but in the main they are well-run establishments that have to be extra careful to keep an orderly house. The police keep a strict watch on such places and if there is any sign of illegal activity, they will rapidly move in and, if they consider it serious, probably challenge the licence.

Another big difference between a gay night-club and one which caters for heterosexuals is the level of violence. Fighting and brawling are almost unknown in gay night-clubs, whereas among the patrons of heterosexual equivalents, aggressive behaviour and serious injury are quite common. The focus in a gay club is less on drunken macho belligerence and more on music, dancing and the pursuit of love. Your son or daughter will probably be safer from injury in a gay night-club than in a mainstream disco.

Gay people generally experience a great sense of liberation and relief when they can let their hair down in congenial surroundings. Their euphoria does not generally show itself in violence and disorder but in fun and good humour. This is not wishful thinking anyone who regularly uses gay pubs and clubs will tell you that violence is extremely uncommon and when it does occur it is usually as a result of harassment from insecure heterosexual youths.

Finding Out For Yourself

Della was worried when she discovered that her son Martin was going to gay night-clubs in London. She had heard stories of drug taking and blatant sexual activity. Her husband had said that no man was safe to go in there alone, and if you went in by accident, you should "keep your back to the wall and don't drop anything on the floor." There had been much raucous laughter when he told this "joke", but she had felt depressed and anxious. What sort of danger was her son exposing himself to in such a place?

When she asked Martin about this, he invited her to come along and find out for herself. She was daunted but resorted to a little trick she had used before when faced with new situations that made her nervous: she asked herself "What's the worst thing that can happen to me if I do this?" She realised that the worst thing that could come out of her visit to the night-club would probably be embarrassment or unease, neither of which are fatal. She took up her son's challenge and, the following Saturday night, went with him:

> I've never been much of a night clubbing sort of person, even in my youth, so I was astonished first of all at the level of noise in this place. The music was deafening, and there was no way you could hold a conversation in there. How people get to know each other with that racket going on, I'll never know.
>
> I was a little shocked at first, seeing men dancing together and women holding on to each other, but I soon got over that. I realised that these were just young people out for a good time on the weekend. I don't particularly like the music they play, to me it's tuneless, but they seem to think it's great. Martin really enjoys dancing, and he danced nearly all night. I had a few dances, too, and I came to realise that I needn't have worried about him. As the night wore on there was a bit of snogging in dark corners, but nothing that you wouldn't see boys and girls doing late at night in the local bus station. Martin didn't even have anything to drink, except a few low-alcohol beers, let alone take drugs. Everyone was quite happy, and I was amazed to see how many friends he had at this club. They all seemed to know him. I was reassured – I'd much rather he was here, wearing himself out dancing, than out doing damage to people and property like so many young people do these days. I've been to the club a couple of times since then, and I've always enjoyed myself, but it's a young people's game and I wouldn't want to go very often.

Another mother who overcame her worries about what goes on in gay bars and clubs was the American writer Mary V. Borhek. She discovered that her son was gay and wrote about the experience in her book *My Son Eric*, (Pilgrim Press, 1979):

> What about gay bars? Aren't they stomach-turning dens of iniquity? Here I must confess that bars – any bars – are not my natural milieu. Straight bars are not my favourite scene, and I have not spent a large portion of my life sitting in them. Of course, there is a wide variation even in straight

bars. Some are fine, but there are also many that I wouldn't care to enter. The same could be said of gay or lesbian bars. Friends have taken me to several, and I can't say I saw anything different going on there from what one sees in a straight bar. The object of the behaviour may be different; for instance two men or two women may be holding hands or standing with their arms around each other, whereas in a straight bar it would be a man and a woman. But the type of behaviour is similar. The friends have not taken me to any of the raunchier gay bars, and I don't care to go to any of those any more than I would care to set foot in a massage parlour, topless bar, or other place that degrades heterosexual sex.

So, should you consider making your own trip to a gay pub or club? Ask yourself, why you want to do it? Are you, like Della, the mother above, trying to reassure yourself that your child is safe to socialise in such places? Or are you just curious to find out a bit more about what gay life is like? The more you find out, the better able you will be to judge whether your child is spending his or her leisure time in reasonable company. Both these reasons are valid, but it is not every gay son or daughter that wants to take his mother or father on to the gay scene: they may be embarrassed or nervous of your reaction. If this is the case, why not ask your son or daughter to get one of their friends to take you along?

It may be, of course, that you won't be made welcome at some establishments. Many gay clubs are jealous of their reputation for providing an exclusively gay environment for their customers and do not welcome "tourists" (as heterosexuals who come on voyeuristic jaunts are called). But if you go along with someone who is already known at the club, it's unlikely that you'll be turned away. You'll find, in the main, that people will be friendly. Gay people often welcome open-hearted heterosexuals into their community and there is even a charming acronym to describe them: HUGS. (Heterosexuals Unafraid of Gays). Most people, I think, would rather be a HUG than a homophobe.

This may all seem out of the question for you at the moment. You may still be struggling with the basic acceptance of your child and declare that stepping into a gay pub is something that you will never do. But you might want to come back to this chapter at some time in the future when your attitudes begin to change a little.

Gay Groups

Where there is no commercial "gay scene" available (in smaller towns and in rural areas), gay people have set up their own alternatives. There is a plethora of non-commercial, self-organised gay groups in Britain, and they play and important role in many people's lives. They also often exist in parallel with gay pubs and clubs, providing and alternative to the frenetic night life. Sitting in pubs which play loud music or staying up half the night in expensive night-clubs is not everyone's idea of a good time. Other people are still shy and uncertain about the wisdom of stepping out of their personal closet, and need something a little more discreet to begin with. Gay groups are often based around the homes of the members, with modest social events such as tea parties, discussion evenings and theatre and cinema outings. Their quiet friendliness suit some people better than the gay scene. Older gay people, who often feel out of place among all the young people in the pubs and clubs, can find a place in gay groups.

As well as the social groups there are "special interest groups", based on hobbies and interests. A quick look through the contact pages of *Gay Times* (the national monthly magazine which is on sale in newsagents throughout the country) will reveal such things as an Acapella Singing Group, a community radio project; Gay Authors Workshop, Gay Gardeners, Gay Linguists, Martial Arts, Vegetarians, Outdoor Adventure Club, Bridge Club, Transport Enthusiasts, Trades Union Groups and so on. Such interest groups have the advantage of providing a focus for people to socialise and get to know one another without the emphasis being too strongly on sex.

Political pressure groups, too, are proliferating within the gay community. As they grow stronger and more confident, gay people are organising themselves to resist the hostility being directed at them. Pressure groups in the areas of AIDS, immigration, parenting and adoption rights, police monitoring and racism are all active. There are groups aimed at influencing the policy of all the main political parties, as well as general lobbying.

The gay community, too, has realised that if it is to see an improvement in the quality of gay life generally, it will have to organise that improvement itself. Consequently there are many support groups, befriending agencies and telephone helplines. Many of these facilities have been in operation for a decade or more and have accumulated a wealth of experience and professionalism in their service delivery.

The AIDS crisis, too, has brought a marvellous response from the gay community, which has created a network of organisations covering every aspect of the disease. When AIDS was seen as "the gay plague", and the government refused to help, gay people were left to their own devices and responded magnificently. They showed the way to the professionals and now gay men are often the real experts in this field and at the forefront of research and social policy.

There are gay religious groups, too, which offer support to the many homosexuals who have strong religious needs — support often denied by the mainstream churches. Consequently, gay organisations have been created to represent just about every religion and denomination you can think of. Gay Jews have several groups, as do Christians, with representation from Quakers, Catholics, Anglicans, Christian Scientists and Mormons. There is even a Gay and Lesbian Humanist Association, for those who want to live their life without any kind of religion at all. For those parents who are having problems with their religious beliefs in relation to their gay son or daughter, Chapter Eight might prove helpful.

The Ghetto Mentality

As you can see, the gay community has flourished and developed in many areas over the last two decades. The wide diversity is well represented and no-one need feel lonely if they are given the chance to find their way around.

But, you might ask, isn't my child going to restrict himself or herself by relying too much on the gay community? Isn't it really just a ghetto that will deny him or her so many opportunities? After all, there are other important things in life, and it can't be healthy to read only gay books or see only gay theatre or eat only at gay restaurants. Isn't it important to integrate into a wide cross section of friends, including heterosexuals?

Some gay people do, for a while, shut themselves away in almost a completely gay world. They mix exclusively with gay people, go only to gay events and shun their heterosexual friends. This is usually a reaction and relief at finding at last what he or she has been searching for. Naturally when gay people first come across such a richness of culture that is so personally relevant to them, they will want to explore it to the full. They have had to endure years of seeing their own experience of life ignored, demeaned or misrepresented, so that when they find a true reflection of their own hopes and aspirations, they will, of course, be exhilarated and want to embrace it fully. This is disturbing to some parents. Here is what one father found when his daughter became a political activist in the lesbian community:

I have come to terms, in most respects, with Linda's sexual preferences, but since she told us about herself she has changed in so many other ways. At one time she was just a normal girl who did the things that you expect your daughter to do. Now she's out and about with all these lesbian women, involved in all kinds of groups. She volunteers on the Lesbian Line counselling service two nights a week, and is part of an encounter group. All these things are making her much more aggressive. Her style of dress has changed, she's now wearing men's jeans and Doc Marten boots, and she's cut her lovely hair off. She's still my daughter, with her beautiful skin and dainty features, but she has adopted this attitude – almost masculine. I find it very disturbing. She told me that she was going on a demonstration, a march through the streets about something or other to do with gay rights. I was worried sick in case she got herself into trouble or got hurt. You see pictures on the news of these demonstrations with people being beaten up and trampled by police horses. I didn't want that to happen to my girl. But I couldn't stop her. I wish I could get her to tone it down a little, I find it embarrassing to be with her in company when she refuses to wear a dress and continues with all this butch clothing. We're a quiet, Jewish family and many of our relatives are very old and very conventional. They don't know how to react to Linda any more. They've stopped asking when she is getting married, although no-one has actually said anything directly about her being a lesbian. I feel we're losing her as she spends more and more time with her homosexual friends.

If, in your opinion, your child is spending too much time with other gay people and exploring all aspects of gay life, then try to be patient and let him or her find their own way at their own pace. Part of this father's problem was not so much that his daughter was gay but that she wanted to do something about it. Her discovery about herself and the subsequent support she was receiving from other women in her community had given her the confidence to be much more her own person, and not try to conform to other people's expectations.

Parents can also feel alienated by the gay community's values and traditions. They have difficulty understanding what motivates such a change of emphasis in their children. The parents who cannot accept their gay child are unlikely to be able to come to terms with that child's chosen way of life. But just because it's different doesn't mean it's bad. And just because it isn't familiar, doesn't mean that you can't deal with it. Consider this, written by psychiatrist Dr. Wayne Dwyer:

> You may have adopted the 'if it's unusual I must stay away from it' mentality, which inhibits your openness to new experiences. Thus, if you see deaf people using sign language, you watch them with curiosity, but never try to converse with them. Similarly when you encounter people who speak a foreign language, rather than work it out and attempt to somehow communicate, you very likely wander off, and avoid the vast unknown of communicating in other than your very own language. There are uncountable people and activities who are considered taboo merely because they are unknown. Thus homosexuals, transvestites, the handicapped, the retarded, nudists and the like are in the category of the obscure. You are not quite certain how to behave, and therefore you avoid the entire business.

Worries about children shutting themselves away exclusively in the gay community are often exaggerated. It would, in any case be difficult for gay people to "ghettoise" themselves in Britain for any length of time. Outside of a few streets in London's Soho, there are few, if any, areas in this country that are exclusively gay — unlike the Castro area of San Francisco where the vast majority of the population is lesbian or gay. The Castro is possibly the only place in the world that could truly qualify as a "gay ghetto" where it is possible to live completely gay with no reference to the outside world.

Ultimately, of course, the only way to discourage the formation of ghettos is to ensure that there is a place for everyone in mainstream society. You can play your part in this by ensuring that your child is a fully functioning and accepted member of the family. You can also encourage a wider acceptance of your child and his or her sexuality. By your example you can teach other people in the extended family, and within your social circle, that acceptance is not only possible but desirable. If your son or daughter doesn't feel excluded from family life, or from society in general, then there is less chance that he or she will want to retire into an exclusive community.

Many gay people find their way from the provinces to London, where it is easier for them to live the kind of life that has a meaning for them. There are more opportunities for finding sympathetic friends, and for socialising, and a better chance of retaining a little anonymity. Those raised in small communities often feel pressured by the community's demands on them to conform; escaping to a big city seems an attractive prospect for such people. Other gay people make good lives for themselves as fully participating members of small communities. They manage to integrate themselves into village life without too much hostility, by being friendly, helpful and by making themselves known as reasonable and likeable individuals.

Going out to work, too, means going into the wider world and into contact with people of all kinds and persuasions. This is Carole, speaking about her son, Jason:

> Jason was the proverbial kid let loose in the sweet shop when he first went on to the gay scene. We live in London, so there is an enormous number of places for him to choose from, and he changes his loyalty like the wind. He likes one club one week and then another the next. He's brought a few of his friends home for me to meet, and I couldn't object to any of them. Lovely people on the whole.
>
> I used to worry constantly about what he was getting up to in the evenings, but I'm not so worried now. I know he has some good friends. The only thing that does trouble me a bit is the amount of gay-bashing that is going on. Gangs of youths will wait outside pubs and clubs for people on their own and then beat them up. I keep telling Jason to get a taxi home and not to walk about on his own. It's such a shame that gay people

can't be left alone to get on with their lives. They aren't doing anyone any harm.

Keep up to date with developments in the gay community by reading the newspapers or magazines which gay people produce for themselves. You'll find details at the back of the book.

Gay Life

Gay life is as diverse and colourful as any other. There are as many ways for gay people to live as there are gay people. Some are happy to remain single, having lots of friends and the occasional lover, others prefer to get into a committed relationship. Some are rich, and live affluent lives in privileged circumstances, others are poor and are forced into low-paid jobs. Some have children, others set great store by their pets.

While the gay scene is busy and lively, many gays prefer to live quiet lives with a circle of close friends. They take no active part in the public expressions of homosexuality and are happy to be discreet.

Perhaps the biggest event of the year in the gay calendar is the Lesbian and Gay Pride Festival, which is held in London on a Saturday towards the end of each June. This has grown from small-scale protest marches in the early seventies into a huge celebration, taking up a whole London park and attracting up to 200,000 people. It is a day when gay people from all over the country gather to make themselves into a force to be reckoned with. Just for once they feel overwhelmingly in the majority. The sense of fun and enjoyment is palpable, and it is an excellent event for parents to attend with their gay sons or daughters. There are equivalent celebrations of Gay Pride in countries throughout the developed world.

This chapter has sought to give a very small introduction to how gay people might live, but as you can see there can be no definitive portrait. Your own son or daughter might choose something entirely different, and live in a way that you may find difficult to understand. So long as they aren't doing anything that is likely to damage themselves or anyone else — abusing drugs, perhaps or becoming dependent on alcohol — the only solution is to be tolerant and to give it time.

We all have to find our own way in the world, and although we might like support from our parents, very few of us want them to interfere to the extent that they try to direct the proceedings. In their book *When Parents Love Too Much* (Century Books, 1990), the authors Laurie Ashner and Mitch Meyerson contend that disappointment with our children can be intensified because we love them too much. They say that perhaps this over-concern with our children's lives can arise because we came from difficult homes ourselves.

An obsession with other people's lives and problems, to the extent that we seldom deal with our own, has been termed co-dependency. Co-dependency is a compulsion to help and control others, and do for them what they could be doing for themselves. Parents who love too much are co-dependent people whose own needs go unmet as they focus all their energy on their children's lives and troubles.

Ashner and Meyerson's solution for parents who are so involved in their children's lives that they become overbearing and manipulative, is to put the focus back on themselves and their own needs. If you find that you always want to know where your child has been, what he or she has been doing, who he or she is seeing, and are always proffering unsolicited advice, then you might need to stop and take a look at what is happening in your own life. Is your own relationship with your spouse or partner stable and fulfilling? Do you have enough social outlets of your own? Do you have interests beyond the family and the doings of your children? If your answer to any of these questions is no, then you might like to think more carefully about what the priorities of your life should be.

Some parents are so concerned about the life their child will lead as a homosexual that their overwhelming concern becomes stultifying. Their doubts and fears express themselves not in direct disapproval, but in more subtle attempts to interfere. Parents often become very adept at manipulating guilt feelings in their children, which might work in the short term, but will eventually cause the child to rebel and become distant.

It's sometimes tricky to decide when our children need our help and intervention and when they need our silence and respect for their privacy. Parents may be concerned that their child is leading a lifestyle that will make them unhappy, but this concern may spring almost entirely from ignorance. The solution is to find a way to remain part of your child's life without actually intruding too much into sensitive areas. Finding out exactly what life is like for gay people can be a great help, and supporting your child in his or her chosen lifestyle will bring its own rich rewards. By trying to understand and providing help and reassurance when necessary, you can build a closer, more adult relationship with your gay son or daughter. As one father revealed:

> When our son told us he was moving in with another man we were shocked, but we decided that the best way to deal with it was to try and help them make it a success. We wanted him to be happy, so we tried not to show him that we were uneasy about the way of life he had chosen. We gave them some furniture to try and make their place look a little less Spartan, and his mother has helped with the curtains and the decorating. We go round there quite often, and we get on with them both. We have never said to our son that we would prefer things to be different – we kept opinions like that to ourselves, and we're glad we did. Actually, we don't feel like that any more. We're both very happy that our son has made such a success of his life with his friend. They have a lovely home, and both have good jobs. We don't interfere in any way and only offer help if it is asked for. It was difficult at first keeping the peace, but we decided between us that it was the best approach. If we'd gone round there like bulls in a china shop, shouting the odds, we would have fallen out and lost him. And that would be a shame because he's a son any parent would be proud of.

7.
How can I help?

The more I looked at it, the more I came to realise how unfairly society treats homosexuals. It made me appreciate my son has to endure. How petty and small-minded it all is. And to think he has to put up with it every day. If I had to live under that kind of pressure I'd go mad, but he copes with it very well. I'm as angry as hell, though, and I'll do whatever I can to make things better.

Although homosexuals have seen dramatic changes for the better in their lives over the past twenty years, there is little doubt that their being honest can still downgrade them in the eyes of a large proportion of the population to the status of second class citizens. As well as having to put up with a daily diet of disapproval, abuse and petty humiliations, they also have to endure discriminatory laws. In theory, everyone is equal before the law but not, it seems, if they're homosexual.

When parents' see this unfairness meted out to their gay sons and daughters as a matter of course, they often become angry and indignant. "How dare they do this to my son?" they ask, or "How can they think this of my daughter?" These feelings of anger are swiftly followed by a sense of helplessness. What on earth can any individual do against such overwhelming odds?

In many ways, accepting your child on his or her own terms and re-integrating this new version into the family is the best help you can give. With such a support system, it is likely that your son or daughter will fare better in a hostile world. If they know they can depend on their loving family when times are rough, the hatred that faces them outside won't seem so formidable. Perhaps the greatest difference you can make to the quality of your child's life is to say and say honestly "We still love you, and we'll defend you when you need us." After all, isn't that what families are for?

The Law

Most countries in the world — even the most progressive — have laws that discriminate against gay people. In Britain there is an unequal age of consent — 16 for heterosexuals, 18 for gay men — and in the United States some states still outlaw gay love. Gay people themselves have gone some way to drawing attention to the iniquity of such legislation and in some instances have managed to get things changed. But they have managed this in the face of ferocious opposition. In Britain this comes from a Right-wing political system and in the United States from fundamentalist religious groups.

Most countries have laws which punish gay men for seeking sexual partners in public places, however discreetly thy may do it. The police will stake out the areas where such activities ("cruising" as it is called in the parlance) take place and sometimes arrest many men at a time. They then have to face the court and the possible wrath of the local community.

But why, you might ask, do people do this? Why don't they find their partners in more dignified and safe places? It's such a sordid business.

We've already looked at a few of the factors that lead some gay men to take risks like this. The pressures they endure to conform and lead a heterosexual life often cause them to marry and try to deny their true feelings. Eventually, in order to find the kind of life they really want, they are forced into encounters in public lavatories, where they hope for anonymity and no complications. There seems to be nowhere else to go. Indeed, a famous piece of research conducted in America by Laud Humphrys (*Tearoom Trade*, Duckworth, 1970) showed that most of the people who resorted to public lavatories to find a sexual outlet did not, in fact, regard themselves as homosexual at all. Most of them were married men with children. The explanation for their activities was that they were seeking sexual outlcts that did not have the complications of emotional commitment (as an affair with a woman would have done), but which were less lonely than masturbation. Men are much more able than women to separate sexual need from the emotional sort. Casual sex means little to most men.

For people driven by loneliness or frustration into these dangerous activities, the consequences of arrest and an appearance in court (and, worse still, the local paper) can be devastating. Public humiliation, rejection by friends and family, often loss of job and the acquisition of a criminal record. All this seems out of proportion to the "crime".

The police, too, are often more zealous about their work in this area than the offence seems to justify. They will often go to elaborate lengths to ensure that they catch men who are "cottaging" (as looking for sex in public lavatories is called). They will drill holes in the wall in order to spy on people using the lavatory, hide in broom cupboards or even on the roof. They also use agent provocateur tactics – posing as gay men and leading others on to making advances before arresting them for "importuning for immoral purposes". Although provoking the commission of a crime is against the policy of most police forces in the civilised world, there are many recorded instances of the police setting out to entrap gay men in public lavatories. Sometimes they will put their youngest and most attractive officers on this duty, dressing them in tight jeans and other provocative clothing. In the gay community these officers are contemptuously known as "the pretty police". It has been asked many times whether these crackdowns on public lavatories are a sensible use of limited police resources. Wouldn't officers be better employed protecting the public from real crimes, where there is a victim: mugging, burglary and car theft?

Homophobia is as common in the police force as it is anywhere else. It's a "man's world" and the pursuit and capture of homosexual "criminals" may be seen seen as a way of proving to your mates that you aren't "one of them". Here is an account of an incident reported in the annual report of the Gay London Police Group (GALOP), which monitors, among other things, police attitudes to gay people, and violence directed at the gay community:

Adrian and his boyfriend were sitting outside the Royal Oak pub in Hammersmith when three police cars pulled up. Nine officers in total emerged, and told the two men to move on. Adrian's boyfriend was tying up his shoelace when one of the officers suddenly pushed him to the ground and began kicking him around the chest and head. He was then arrested and taken to the local police station. The custody officer despatched him to Charing Cross hospital, where seven stitches were recommended. The officer in charge insisted that there was an urgent need to get back to the police station, and so a temporary bandage was applied. Back at the police station, a charge of being drunk and disorderly was made against Adrian's boyfriend, who accepted the caution, not realising that this was tantamount to an admission of guilt.

Gay people also complain about the lack of interest shown by the police in violence that is directed at the gay community. Here is another case from the GALOP report:

Derek and Tim were walking through Islington late at night when they were approached by two men, one of whom asked them for a light. Moments later they were being beaten with what they believe was a wooden club, both receiving various injuries to the head and upper torso. Derek needed twenty stitches in his forehead. They reported the attack to the local police who, they say, were polite but did not seem particularly interested.

Lesbians are also subjected to discrimination in the law. Any lesbian woman who has a child from a previous heterosexual marriage could lose custody if she is challenged on the grounds of her lesbianism. As we've already seen, there is no evidence to show that a child would be disadvantaged by being raised by a lesbian mother – or a gay father – but still courts frequently deprive gay people of their parental rights simply because they are gay.

In Britain, those concerned with civil liberties (both gay and straight) were very angry about the introduction, in 1988, of Section 28 of the Local Government Act. This clause bans the "deliberate promotion of homosexuality in schools". It was introduced after Right-wing politicians tried to convince the country that homosexual propaganda was being fed to children in schools. To the people who proposed this clause, "propaganda" consists of any positive image of homosexuals. They still cling to the theory that, unless it is discouraged, children go through a phase of homosexual experimentation, will turn into 'permanent homosexuals'. As we've already seen, basic sexual orientation is probably fixed at a very early age, long before a child goes to school. The idea that they can be proselytised into a homosexual orientation flies in the face of all known facts. It is true that some children experiment with each other homosexually, but for most this is more to do with curiosity than any permanent change of sexual identity. For the substantial minority of those children that have a homosexual orientation, some positive images are likely to be very important indeed. If they were offered some information about homosexuality that would give them reassurance, then they might be spared many years of anguish. Remember, they will have realised they are 'different', potentially despised, but unlike other minorities – like racial or religious ones – they will have no support from their families.

The worst that positive images can do to those children who are not homosexual is to challenge their prejudices. Maybe, as a result, we would have a new generation that did not share its parents' hatred of gay people.

But such is the depth of homophobia in our society that these messages penetrate very slowly indeed. Whatever social scientists say to the contrary, the myths and stereotypes cling on tenaciously. The availability of objective research has had minimal impact against the lies that are daily peddled about homosexuals and homosexuality.

In the end, Section 28 was so badly thought out and so illogically drafted that it is unenforceable, but that does not mean it has been entirely ineffective in making life difficult for gay people. By passing through Parliament, Section 28 made it clear that the Government of Britain still does not regard homosexual people as deserving of equal rights and protection. In fact it even refers to homosexual couples as living in "pretend family relationships" – something which many gay people find grossly insulting. The Section has also given an excuse to local authorities to restrict grants to gay initiatives, such as counselling agencies, AIDS education projects and artistic endeavours. Even though Section 28 does not prevent the giving of grants to gay voluntary groups, some local authorities have said that they don't want to risk prosecution. A perfect escape clause for those who are homophobic, but don't want to say so publicly.

Public Money And Homosexuality

There has been much controversy about the giving of grants by local authorities to gay projects. The conservative press uses the issue relentlessly to discredit those authorities who hold a different political opinion to their own. However worthy the cause may be (and a helpline for distressed gay people is as worthy, surely, as a helpline for anyone else), the newspapers constantly suggest that gay people don't deserve any share of the money that is annually granted to voluntary groups by local authorities. Why is this? Don't gay people living in a given area have to pay local taxes? Of course they do! But they are often denied the benefits which are supposed to accrue from their substantial contributions.

The reason local authorities make grants to voluntary groups is because, in the end, it saves them much more than they spend. If specialist support groups, manned by volunteers, did not exist, the council's social services would have to take on the work that they do. And that would be a much more expensive proposition.

The amount of money given to gay organisations from the public purse is tiny, but they are excellent value for money. If a gay helpline can persuade only two or three people not to attempt suicide, then they will have saved the Health Service a small fortune. They will also have prevented a lot of unhappiness.

Discrimination Is Widespread

Other discriminations are many and varied. In almost every area of life, gay people may possibly find themselves disadvantaged. In housing, employment, immigration, family life, and even walking down the street. The emergence of AIDS has not helped. Indeed, the disease has given people a new excuse for their hatred and prejudice and seems to have fired a further backlash.

Gay people are still losing their jobs because of their sexuality. There is no legal protection, and little sympathy in industrial tribunals. Although some trades unions are introducing policies to protect their gay members from discrimination, there can be no guarantee that they will have any effect upon unfair treatment. Often gay people are dismissed for reasons that are difficult to pin down, they are told they are "unsuitable" or that their colleagues find them difficult to get on with. As Paul Crane put it, in his book *Gays and The Law* (Pluto Press, 1985):

There is no legislation [in Britain] to protect gay women and men in employment. Employers may therefore refuse to hire, refuse to promote and may even dismiss or demote gay employees solely on the grounds of common prejudice. Fellow workers sometimes make complaints to employers which lead to dismissal. In this situation, gay workers are doubly handicapped, having neither the protection of law nor support from their workmates.

The Campaign for Homosexual Equality published a leaflet entitled *Queers Need Not Apply* which contained the following anecdote:

A woman teacher, whose new employers were somewhat slow in completing the normal formalities, had been working for two months when she was informed that she was 'medically unfit' to teach. She had mentioned in completing her medical history form that she was suffering from a mild form of depression. She told us: 'After some investigations, I discovered that from my GP had revealed that my mild depression was due to marital troubles as a consequence of my having had lesbian affairs.' She confronted her occupational health officer, who told her: 'A lesbian cannot be trusted in a girls' school, where some of the girls are quite well developed.' The same fears, however, did not apply to the employment of male teachers in the same girls' school, for heterosexual men were 'not in question'. Had the school been more prompt in contacting her GP, of course, the case would not have arisen, for she would have been rejected as unsuitable from the outset, for reasons which she would not have known.

Homosexuality, too, still provides grounds for dismissal from the Armed Forces. So strong is the resistance to reform in this area that in the Unites States it severely damaged the standing of the President when he tried to make reforms. In Britain, the military hierarchy is profoundly opposed to the acceptance of gay and lesbian service-people.

As well as being drummed out of the Forces in disgrace, soldiers and sailors, air force personnel (male and female) can quite easily be deprived of their pension entitlement and other benefits, if they are found to be homosexual.

One woman, Elaine Chambers, who completed five years and ten months' service in the Queen Alexandra Nursing Corps, was forced to resign her commission after the Army's Special Investigations Bureau (SIB) searched her room and discovered enough evidence to "convict" her of being a lesbian. The report of her case, in *The Independent* (12 June, 1991) told the whole story:

> The allegations against Elaine were not just that she was a lesbian. She had been accused of indecently assaulting two fellow officers. She had a 'one-night stand' with one woman and a 'necking session' with another. But each time, Elaine was able to prove, the involvement was consenting. It is an indication of the fear that an SIB investigation can arouse that two friends in the nursing corps could accuse her of assaulting them in an effort not to get themselves into trouble. Elaine's innocence of the assault charges was proved at her 15-hour interrogation the Monday after her room was searched. The questioning was detailed. At one stage she was asked about distinguishing features on the body of the woman she had slept with. At a second, nine-hour, interrogation she was quizzed about other women in the services whose names appeared in her letters and diaries. Eventually five other women were compelled to leave the armed services as a result of follow-up investigations. One was medically discharged as suffering from a psychiatric breakdown.

It is unlikely that openly gay people would be allowed to hold senior diplomatic posts. The reasons given by the Government for this discrimination is that gay people would be open to blackmail in these sensitive positions. It has been known in the past for gay men to be blackmailed into passing on State secrets after being compromised by enemy agents. The argument, however, is circular. If gay people have identified themselves as such, it follows that no-one can blackmail them by threatening to expose them – they've already done it themselves. On the other hand, those gay people who hide the truth about themselves might well pass through the vetting procedure, but they are the ones who are open to blackmail because they are desperate not to lose their jobs.

This simple logic is lost on the powers-that-be in the British civil service.

A survey by The Gays and Housing Group found that one person in five who contacted Lesbian and Gay Switchboard with a housing problem said their homelessness was connected with their gayness. All kinds of complications can arise for two people of the same sex who want to share a home. Local authorities won't always allow joint tenancies to such couples or, if a same-sex couple do manage to share a council flat, the remaining partner might be evicted if the named leaseholder dies.

What You Can Do To Help Your Child

Until their child comes out as gay, many parents have no idea what life is like for homosexuals in this country. Like just about everybody else, they don't think about it because they don't regard it as having anything to do with them. But when it does become "something to do with them", they are appalled at the pettiness and vindictiveness of some of the acts of discrimination. They are angered by the spite and malice which is directed at people just like their own son and daughter. They are stunned by the sheer volume of the hatred.

Some of them become so angry that they are determined to join the struggle for gay rights, and they do it in a number of ways. Some of them take their lead from their son or daughter. They ask: "How can I help you, how can I do my bit to make things better?"

This is what happened to Edmund when his daughter Kathy was hit in the face by a man as she came out of a gay club:

I couldn't believe it. She wasn't doing any harm to anyone, she'd just been for a night out with her friends. But there was this gang of yobs waiting outside the club. When Kathy and her mates left, they were jeered at and harassed by these youths. Kathy tried to push past them, and one of them punched her in the face for no reason. She had an enormous black-eye when she got home, but she didn't complain. I was so upset, though, that I went to bed and cried. How could anyone do that to her? She's a lovely girl, and she doesn't deserve to be treated like that.

When Kathy reported the incident to the police they were uninterested. It may have been that they were overwhelmed with work that evening, but Edmund suspects that because it happened outside the gay club, the police ignored the matter.

Eventually he decided that the only way to get things changed was to challenge the police directly. He asked to see the Chief Inspector at the local police station, and discussed the matter with him. That meeting proved unsatisfactory, so he eventually wrote a letter to the local paper. The editor was so interested that he turned it into a full-scale feature, which in turn led to the local police making a promise that they would investigate all crimes of violence, wherever they happened and whoever was the victim. They refused to accept that gay people were treated differently.

Gay-bashing is a nasty business and is the ultimate expression of homophobia. On some occasions it has even proved fatal. If your son or daughter is a victim of this kind of violence (which can take milder but still very distressing forms, too, such as bullying at work), then you can offer support and practical assistance in pursuing claims for compensation and ensuring that justice is done.

When parents are seen to speak out publicly it has an amazing effect on public perceptions of the struggle for gay rights. No longer can "ordinary" people dismiss protests about anti-gay discrimination as special pleading by a tiny, irrelevant minority. They find it easier to identify with other parents, and see the whole thing in a different light. Some might, of course, think 'there but for the grace of God go I', others will feel a spark of empathy and maybe even change their opinions a little.

Some parents have appeared on radio and television programmes talking about their experiences with their gay son or daughter. Others have given interviews to newspapers and magazines. They have all hoped that their contribution would somehow lessen the burden that their children have to carry. Betty Boswell, for instance, gave an interview to Robert Kilroy-Silk which appeared in *The Sunday Mirror* Magazine (16 June, 1991), telling of her own experiences when her 17-year old son Glyn:

> It took me a couple of years to get to grips with it fully, to the point where I could say 'My son's homosexual and this is his partner Richard — I regard him as my son-in-law.' My husband Ron, once he came round, was very supportive...But

your son is still your son, no matter what. If you're a parent who's just found out, the greatest help is realising that you're not the only one."

Betty has since put her own experience to good use and is involved in an organisation for parents of homosexuals called Acceptance.

But not everyone wants to be politically active, or publicly identified as the parent of a gay person, although they still want to do something. Denise was one such person, who was angered when her local vicar delivered a vehemently anti-gay sermon. She sat in the pew listening to the fire and brimstone condemnation of homosexuals:

I felt myself shrivelling up as I listened to the vicar's words. I couldn't bring myself to look round the congregation because I imagined that everyone would be looking at me, knowing that I was the mother of a gay son — a dreadful sinner according to the vicar. But the more I listened, the angrier I became. My shame turned into a desire to defend my son. When I got home I rang the vicar and told him that I had been deeply hurt by his words, which I thought were uncharacteristically cruel and hard. He tried to justify himself, but I wouldn't have it. I demanded that he let me write an article in the Parish Magazine, putting the other side of the story. He wasn't too pleased at that idea, but I said that if he didn't allow me to have my say, I was going to leave the church. And I meant it. He said he would think about it and call me back. Well, he did, and he agreed that I could write my article. When it was published, my name was there at the bottom for everyone to see. The Sunday following the publication of the parish magazine, I was very nervous about going to church, but I had to go and show them that what I'd said was true. I wasn't ashamed of my son, and I didn't think there was any contradiction between his life and my faith. When I got there, one of the women members of the congregation came up to me and shook my hand. She said she thought I'd been very courageous. She said she hoped she would have as much courage if she was in the same situation. I didn't get any bad reactions at all.

I don't regret doing anything, but I must admit that I've drawn away from the church a bit since it all happened. I'm on cool terms with the vicar, and only go to church about once a month now. I feel I can keep the faith in my own way, without having to go against the dictates of my conscience.

Most parents, though, simply do their best in day to day life, either supporting their children through the difficult times or taking a small personal stand whenever and wherever it seems necessary. They want to influence, if they can, the way society reacts to homosexuals. They want to reduce the discrimination, and they speak with a unique authority. In America the parents' of gays are well aware of their influential position and exploit it to the full. Their deputations to meet politicians, church leaders and others who are hostile to their sons and daughters, are extremely powerful. British parents have made a start, but they are not yet organised in quite the same way.In the end, most just want their child to be happy. If that means becoming involved in politics, then they'll do it. Most achieve it in a quieter way, supporting their own child as and when necessary. When they have overcome their shock, most parents of gay people become accepting. The greatest gift they can give their child. After years of possibly suicidal isolation, the emerging gay person can at last be free to grow. You can release your child from the misery of denial and lies simply by saying 'I still love you, even though you aren't who I thought you were.'

This concept of emergence was expressed very well by Marshall Kirk and Hunter Madsen in their book *After The Ball* (Plume Books, 1989):

So it turns out that, while a majority of gays are as well adjusted and content as straights, a sizable minority of homosexuals are deeply unhappy. Straights generally suppose that homosexuality itself is to blame for this. Gays, on the other hand, insist quite rightly that what makes them unhappy is the way straights treat them. The entire situation reminds one of *The Ugly Duckling*, the fairy tale in which a despairing young swan learns to hate itself because its odd appearance has elicited ridicule and scorn from the ducks into whose company it has fallen. That touching tale was penned by Hans Christian Andersen. Andersen, as it happens, was himself a particularly effeminate gay man who probably knew a thing or two about the unhappiness produced by social rejection. Fortunately for the cygnet in the story. it grows up to become a majestic trumpeter, leaves the astonished (and, ultimately, admiring) ducklings behind, and joins the grand company of others like itself. The swan lives happily ever after. But that's a fairy tale. In the real world, many gays grow up feeling ugly and scorned, and continue to feel that way as adults.

You can help your child to emerge from his or her ugly duckling status and become a proud swan, simply by refusing to subscribe to the ignorant nonsense which most people believe to be the truth about homosexuality.

What Does The Future Hold?

Are things getting better or worse for gay people ask parents. Is life becoming easier or harder for my son or daughter?

As with all large-scale social changes, the fight for homosexual rights is a long, bitter and frequently bumpy one. The gay community itself lurches from depression to euphoria as battles are won and lost. One day a major advance will be achieved but then this seems to be wiped out by some unbelievable backward step. It seemed, for instance, that gay equality was within grasp in the early seventies the law had been changed, social acceptance was increasing. The along came AIDS, and the clock was brutally reversed. But campaigners will tell you that even AIDS has brought benefits in the struggle for homosexual emancipation. It has forced the subject to be acknowledged in circles where it was always denied. It has forced those who were indifferent to take a stand.

In the early days of the AIDS epidemic, homosexuals appeared to be obtaining again the status of pariah. Opinion polls showed that public disapproval of gay lifestyles was at its highest since the law had been changed. But that is beginning to change again. Little by little, gay people are feeling once more that things are moving their way.

As one gay activist put it:

It seems to be a case of two steps forward and one step back. It's a long, slow process. The strange thing is, though, that the more aggression we have directed at us, the stronger we seem to become. Despite the fact that AIDS is supposed to have shoved us back into the closet, there are more openly gay people nowadays than there have ever been. I remember going to the London gay pride march back in 1972. There were about 2,000 people on that. We thought it was amazing that so many gay people should gather together in one place at the same time. Nowadays 100,000 isn't unusual. Every time the Government does something like introduce Section 28, gay people get angrier and more determined to fight back. All attempts to make us invisible seem just to make us more determined to come out. Gay life is in flux at the moment. But I think in the end we'll get there. It's going to be a hard slog, though, and we're going to have to fight every one of the battles.

Certainly the gay rights agenda seems to have moved to a very prominent position in the struggle for human rights generally. It seems that there is some development almost every day, and newspaper articles and television programmes raise the profile much higher. This is bound to create a reaction from those who are implacably opposed to the integration of gay people into every day life. We see it in the way politicians use homosexuality as a tool to score points for themelves, and the way that the religious right in the United States is organising to attempt once more to turn gay people into pariahs and outcasts. But this cynical politicking with peoples' lives is wicked and ultimately destined to fail. Unfortunately, many will be hurt before that time comes.

Some parents will want to be part of the battle, and some will want to simply offer encouragement from the sidelines. But despite the occasional setback and bout of pessimism, the future for gay people looks better than it has ever done before.

8.
Religion and culture

Parents may believe that they must choose between their daughter or son and the Church. An adult child's self-revelation may set off a religious and spiritual crisis in the family as the parents struggle to reconcile the Church's judgement with their own knowledge of their child's goodness...Relatives of gays/lesbians may use the Church's teaching as a moral club with which to berate their gay/lesbian relation in the hopes of effecting change. Some families similarly use the Church's teaching as a reason to sever all ties with the gay relative, or as a reason to be ignorant about the gay relative's life. The Church's teaching, therefore, easily becomes one more source of conflict and tension between gay men, lesbians and their families. — Clark, Brown, Hochstein, *Institutional Religion and Gay/Lesbian Oppression* (Harrington Press, 1990).

As many parents have discovered, a strong religious commitment does not automatically mean that you can never accept or support your gay child. There is no doubt, though, that for some people, it can be one of the most intractable barriers standing between them and their homosexual son or daughter. There are many people for whom Christian faith and homosexuality are simply incompatible. For them, the discovery of a gay child within their family can be so catastrophic that they are totally unable to progress beyond their initial rejection. This was illustrated in the story of one gay man, David Lewis, a committed Christian who worked in a Residential Centre. He wrote about his experience with his traditionally religious parents in *Christian Action Journal* (Summer 1990):

"Only six weeks before, my mother had happened on one of (my boyfriend Paul's) letters to me: a beautiful letter, expressing his longing to be in my company, explaining how much he loved me, and how important I was to him — with the odd bit of quirky humour, here and there: teasing me, in the way only people on intimate terms may.

Of course, my mother, from whom, up till then, I had kept hidden that I was gay, did not find the letter in the least bit amusing. And, of course, she shouldn't have read it. If I'd wanted her to find out I was homosexual, I'd have preferred to have told her in person: but I hadn't wanted to upset her. Never before, as far as I'd known, had she visited my home in the Residential Centre without informing me in advance. On this particular occasion I was away. She'd told the staff she was popping in to make herself a cup of tea. She hadn't been able to resist reading the letter, which was lying on my desk in my study. She'd returned home and reported the matter to my father, who then informed me what had happened.

My indignation rendered me speechless. My parents, I was told, would have nothing more to do with me. What's more I was to be reported to the church "authorities", as I was obviously unfit to be in charge of a Residential Centre. No boy could be safe in my care. How could they — decent Christians — have raised such a pervert?

Argument was fruitless. My previously good relationship with my parents was destroyed. The more I tried to reason with my father, the more stubborn he became.

'Would you have thought that girls were in danger if I were heterosexual?' I asked him.

'Of course not,' he replied.

'So why...?'

'It's a perversion...It's not natural.'

'Well, it's natural for me. This is the way I've been made, and, if we're going to take the concept of God as Creator seriously, then...'

'Don't bring God into it!'

'But I've spent many hours on my knees praying about this, and, as far as I'm concerned, being a homosexual doesn't come in the way of my relationship with God. He loves me the way I am!'

'Well, your mother and I don't any more...I can arrange for you to see a psychiatrist.'

'But I'm not ill. Please talk to someone about it — perhaps an understanding priest — so that you can get their point of view.'

'There's nothing I need to know more about. It's an abomination...To think my own son...'

'But I'm still the same person you used to admire and think the world of.'

'Not any more.'

Not any more. Not any more. I'd lost the love and respect of my parents...Why, I'd have to find out."

Despite the often irrational and, some would say cruel, reactions of individual members, many churches and denominations are in flux on this issue. Modern insights and thinking have made it far from straight-forward for many religious leaders. Some, like the Quakers, seem to be at peace with their gay brethren, others, like the Catholics are still adamant that homosexuality is unacceptable. Perhaps the document that expresses the "official" Roman Catholic stance most clearly is *On the Pastoral Care of Homosexual Persons* written by Cardinal J. Ratzinger and approved by Pope John Paul II. The thesis of this pastoral letter is that homosexual behaviour is not a "morally acceptable option" and that even the inclination towards homosexual behaviour is a "more or less strong tendency towards an intrinsic moral evil."

When it was published, this letter caused a furore because of its harsh and uncompromising stance. Like so much of present Catholic doctrine on social issues, it is often ignored by individual Catholics who cannot accept Pope John Paul II's rigid pronouncements on a whole range of difficult subjects. Before this document was issued, many Catholic theologians had begun to reach a more compassionate conclusion, and even now there is a substantial body of opinion within the Church that does not accept its present stance. But these dissenters must disagree quietly and privately or risk censure.

In the study mentioned at the beginning of this chapter, the researchers Clark, Brown and Hochstein said of current Catholic policy:

"It is important to note that this official position is not unchangeable, infallible teaching. It is simply the current doctrinal position of Roman Catholicism. Because it is not infallible, it contains the theoretical possibility of error and is ideally open to change and correction. Although the Church certainly does not encourage or support dissent or dialogue about doctrinal matters among its faithful, such dissent and dialogue continue. Although the official Church widely disseminates and quotes this document, the Church is not monolithic. Less vocal, less public theologians view a homosexual orientation and sexual behaviour as valid Christian possibilities and perceive gay men and lesbians as good, healthy people who are open to the grace of God."

The Church of England continues to debate the issue, and it has become a matter of great controversy for Anglicans. The Archbishop of Canterbury has admitted that he is still struggling with the problems of gay people within the church and has reached no conclusion. Indeed, in 1990 the Church of England suppressed a report which it had commissioned (The Osborne Report) because it was almost wholly supportive of lesbian and gay people within the Church. The issue seems to be causing mighty upheaval in the Church of England and will continue to do so for many years to come.

Less traditional denominations, with evangelical or fundamentalist philosophies, opposed any acceptance of homosexuality and cite Biblical teaching as the final word on the matter. Some of these fundamentalist churches not only refuse to accept homosexuality as a valid way of life, they actually campaign vigorously to ensure that there is no place for gay people anywhere in society. They have declared open war against homosexual people and carry out these hostilities with an unflagging energy. They campaign furiously to prevent reforms in the law or against fairer treatment for gay people in other areas. Those fundamentalist preachers in the USA with political ambitions are exploiting the supposed biblical hostility to homosexuality to further their own quest for power. The result is that prejudice and discrimination are further fuelled, and cruelty towards and mistreatment of lesbian and gay people inevitably follows.

Religious attitudes over the centuries have been the source of most of the prejudice which attends gay people today. Although it sometimes feels that there is a move towards acceptance and understanding of gay people within the religious community, there are frequent set-backs. You don't have to look very far to find violently expressed denouncements of homosexuality from some religious people, and so I will not repeat them here. Instead, I will give this chapter over to the other point of view. If you are struggling to find a way to accommodate your child's homosexual orientation with your strongly-held religious beliefs, then it will be helpful for you to know that there are other ways of looking at the matter. If you are unwilling to even listen to these other arguments, then perhaps there is little hope of your progressing to a full understanding of what is going on in the life of your gay child. If, though, your heart is open and your mind still free of a dogmatic straitjacket, let us see what others have to say.

First I will turn to an Anglican vicar, the Reverend Neil Richardson, whose parish is in a west London borough. He is heterosexual, and also a serving member of the local council. The council introduced an equal opportunities policy which promised that people from ethnic minorities, women, the disabled and lesbians and gays would not be discriminated against in employment with the authority. The council also made clear that it was supportive of disadvantaged minorities — including lesbians and gays — in other areas of life.

When this policy was announced, a number of fundamentalist Christians in the borough were outraged and formed an opposition group aimed at getting the council to dismantle the policy — at least as far as lesbians and gay men were concerned. This they eventually achieved.

Mr Richardson was saddened by the activities of these fellow Christians and was moved to write a small pamphlet refuting the literalism of the fundamentalist group. He has given me permission to quote from the pamphlet at length, and I hope that those of you who are wrestling with the problem of what the Bible says, and what your child is, will find some comfort in this alternative way of looking at biblical teaching:

"Much of the impetus for the opposition to the Council's policy comes from a small and unrepresentative group of fundamentalist Christians, whose reading of the Bible is narrow, literalistic and pre-scientific. It harks back over 100 years and utterly ignores all advances in knowledge which have taken place in the twentieth century, and not only knowledge about human beings, gained through psychology, psychiatry and sociology, but they reject advances in biblical knowledge that have helped theologians and scholars interpret the ancient writings of the Jews and Christians for the modern world. These fundamentalists are, I am sure, deeply sincere people, but that doesn't make then right. And how sad it is to see an attempt to saddle and harness the sincerity of these people by certain politicians whose cynical manipulation of the subject demonstrates the emptiness of their own store of political ideas.

When you read the Bible without the benefit of modern theological tools and without a bit of common sense, it becomes a happy hunting ground for cranks and eccentrics of all kinds. Of course if you just flip through the bits that refer to homosexuality without due regard for the context and understanding of the community for which the passages were originally written, you will come away in no doubt that homosexual relations are condemned. But if you read with insight and understanding, you may find a very different interpretation possible.

First of all, we must remember that the Bible was written a long time ago, and in a world that was very different to ours. It was written over a long period of time — over 1,000 years — and some of the older parts have an oral pre-history of even greater antiquity. The one thing which all these periods have in common is that they were all 'paternalistic' societies in which the dominance of the male over the female and the economic dependence of women on men was presumed to be natural and God-given. Women were seen as secondary to men, as is evidenced by the story of creation of Eve from the rib of Adam in Genesis 2:21-23, and many other incidents in the Bible in which women are portrayed as the property of men, and having less honour in the order of things. We must remember that the Bible describes life and times which were brutal and crude in the main, and in which death, war and disease were often seen as signs of God's displeasure. The Jewish writers whose work we describe as The Old Testament were not, in the majority of cases, writing to describe private life and issues, but trying to interpret the events of history for the Jewish community. They were asking the question: how faithful has Israel been to the Covenant with God? And they looked for the answers in the affairs of the Court and the Kings and leaders. I doubt very much if even the idea of a stable and loving gay relationship had ever crossed the minds of these ancient writers, including those whose writings refer to homosexuality. The context in which they wrote to condemn was one of religions which indulged in 'cultic prostitution' – an aspect of the religions of the agrarian communities existing in the middle east in biblical times. In this context, we may agree that homosexual relations are properly condemned. But condemned because they do not have a loving and fulfilling purpose for those who participate.

The most famous passage in the Bible which is quoted on this subject is Genesis 19:4-11 (the story of Sodom and Gomorrah). It is a strange and ancient passage and its meaning is obscure. Traditionally, it has been understood as a reference to homosexuality – hence the name 'sodomite' – because of the phrase in verse 5: "that we may know them". The inference is that the crowd outside Lot's house wish to homosexually molest the two men inside who Lot has befriended and offered hospitality. To make this passage into a reference to homosexuality, it is necessary to interpret the verb 'to know' to mean have 'carnal' knowledge. (The Hebrew word is transliterated into English as *yada*.) However, there are compelling reasons for refuting this interpretation.

1. The verb *yada* can mean 'to know' in a variety of ways, and not just the sexual connotation. (e.g. Genesis 3:5 'For God doth know that in the day ye eat thereof...'; Genesis 27:2 'And he said, behold now, I am old, I know not the day of my death.' etc.). In these, and many other examples, the verb *yada* or 'to know' is the verb used. To translate *yada* in this context as meaning 'carnal knowledge' is to have already entered into a stage of interpretation of what the writer meant when originally he wrote it. In no sense can this passage be understood as unambiguously referring to homosexual intercourse, and there are further reasons for thinking it is, in fact, an incorrect interpretation to do so.

2. Genesis 19: verse 4 shows that 'all people, both young and old, from every quarter' were gathered round Lot's house, calling for the two men. That would include women and children and, in those circumstances, it is unlikely that a homosexual rape would take place.

3. Most telling of all, perhaps, is that the subsequent references in the Old Testament to the 'sin of Sodom' do not refer to

homosexuality. For example, read Ezekiel 16:49-50 where the sin of Sodom is described as 'pride, fullness of bread, prosperous ease was in her daughters, neither did she strengthen the hand of the poor or needy...' This passage goes on to mention 'committing abomination' but this must be seen as a reference to worshipping at the shrines of false gods. (Compare Ezekiel 7:20 or 44:13.)

The Genesis 19 story of Sodom and Gomorrah depends on the presence of two 'angels' who, in Hebrew thought, represent the presence of God. Thus when you read the story with understanding you see that it is a condemnation of an inappropriate relationship with God. The people of Sodom are guilty of selfishness and a failure to be properly hospitable, to reflect the generosity of God, and freely express this in their social relations, and treatment of aliens, strangers and the underprivileged.

The sin of Sodom may be summed up as 'inhospitality', meaning the improper use of God's goodness, which should be shared by all. The irony of the interpretation is brought out in the following quotation:

'For thousands of years in the Christian West, the homosexual has been the victim of inhospitable treatment. Condemned by the Church, he has been the victim of persecution, torture, and even death. In the name of a mistaken understanding of Sodom and Gomorrah, the true crime of Sodom and Gomorrah has been, and continues to be repeated every day.' (From *The Church and The Homosexual* by Fr. J.J. McNeill).

A casual reading of the first few verses of Genesis 19 may give the impression that homosexuality is involved, but if you read from chapter 17, through to the end of chapter 19, you get a taste of the complexity and ultimately, the mystery of the passages which reflect ancient culture, and have nothing to say to us about homosexuality. Note how in chapter 17, it is 'the Lord who appears to Abram'. By chapter 18:2 it is 'three men' and by chapter 19:1 it is 'two angels'. This is an ancient piece of literature which has great subtlety and a complex pre-history, but quite obviously, it teaches us nothing on this subject, and it is very sad that much of the Church's understanding of homosexuality has been disfigured by a superficial understanding of Genesis 19.

If you wish to take a literalistic reading of any parts of the Bible, you must acknowledge that you have been involved in a process of interpretation and there is no such thing as 'what the Bible says' but only an interpretation of what the Bible says.

Admittedly there are passages which show that ancient civilisations condemned homosexual relations. For example, Leviticus 18:22 is clear: 'Thou shalt not lie with mankind as with womankind.' Anxiety about homosexual relations have always been present in society. That is not in doubt. What is in doubt is the possibility that those who condemned homosexual activity really understood it as we do today. What they lacked was a perspective on what it is like to be a homosexual, whether male or female, who finds deeply satisfying and fulfilling human relationships through same-sex love.

What has influenced me in my personal approach to this issue has been the very real love which I have seen gay friends sharing together. The integrity of their love and relationships taught me that it is wrong to condemn. They have something of great value: they love each other, and in a world where there is little enough love to go round. So why oppose this love when it is obviously productive of personal growth, happiness and fulfilment? And when it has made a contribution to the whole community? I could not ever, in the light of my experience of gay friends, simply quote Leviticus 18:22 to condemn them. And why should Leviticus 18:22 be taken quite so literally? Why not take equally seriously Leviticus 17:10? Leviticus 17:10 forbids the eating of meat which has not been drained of blood. Why do not Christian Fundamentalists equally condemn those who eat their Sunday joint? Are they all Kosher? Of course they are not. Their giving weight to one particular part of scripture is typical of the pitfalls of fundamentalism. In the end, it shows clearly that we must bring to our reading of the Bible our God-given ability to interpret the ideas of the past with modern insights, and where necessary, reject the culture-bound ideas in the Bible in our discussion of what our modern attitudes should be.

The fundamentalists may turn to the New Testament for more ammunition to fight against homosexuality. At first sight, there is more hope of anti-gay material here. However, it is worth nothing that there are no references to homosexuality in the Gospels, and Jesus is not known to have referred to it to condemn, either as an orientation, or as a genital activity. If it had been a major issue, we might have expected him to comment. The main source for our fundamentalists comes from the writings of Saint Paul, and especially in Romans 1:18-22. There are things about this passage which must be looked at carefully. First, Paul is deeply concerned about how pagan religion is affecting Christianity. He was right to be worried, for Rome and Corinth and other major cities were hot-beds of exploitation of many kinds, and where, under the name of 'religion', various unattractive activities, including sexual activities, were found. Paul refers to homosexual acts, in Romans 1, as arising out of idolatry and it is clear from the context that it is idolatry he is condemning. When he uses the word 'nature' in Romans 1:26, he speaks of those of a heterosexual orientation who, as part of pagan rituals, change to homosexual acts. While we may all agree that this kind of pagan practice is worthy of condemnation, it is hard to read into this passage, a general condemnation of what we now understand as adult, same-sex loving relationships. The situation and conditions in which homosexual love takes place are quite different. Further, many homosexuals see their orientation as part of their true 'nature' and so they are, in fact, not contravening Paul's words, because they are responding positively to what they perceive as 'natural for them'. In these terms, it is those who try to persuade homosexuals to become heterosexual who are contravening the spirit of what Paul says in Romans 1.

Even if you take a fundamentalist view of Romans 1, you must be careful again not to be selective in how you read. Paul condemns homosexual acts as 'worthy of death' but if you read a little further back in the chapter he similarly condemns 'unrighteousness, wickedness, covetousness, maliciousness, envy, murder, strife, deceit, malignity, whisperers, backbiters and the unmerciful, etc.' (Romans 1:29-30). Are we to take this as a yardstick for modern attitudes?

In the end, what sense does it make to simply take the writings of Paul from the 1st century AD and regurgitate them for use today? Paul was a man of his time, and his commentary on social issues merely reflects the common assumptions of his day. So, when he writes about women, he assumes that 'the husband is the head of the wife...' (Ephesians 5:23). This doctrine of 'male headship' underpins Paul's understanding of men and women. Women are therefore advised to submit to their husbands. Clearly, Paul's teaching reflects the social reality of his own day and age, and cannot be taken to commit the church today on its teaching on the subject of marriage. In 1 Timothy 2:8-15, Paul teaches that 'women are saved through childbearing' and he forbids women to 'teach or have dominion over a man.' As evidence for this, he returns to the creation of Eve from Adam's rib. Any true fundamentalist will, therefore, not only take exception to the Council's policy as it applies to gay and lesbian people, but will be forced, by the internal logic of their own position, to condemn Equal Opportunities for women and girls as equally contrary to biblical precepts.

Paul taught that all sexual relations were best avoided. 'It is good for a man not to touch a woman.' (1 Corinthians 7:1). He only allowed sexual contact as a sop to the weakness of those who, unlike himself, were unable to remain celibate. His views on this, as indeed, on many subjects, were held in the light of his understanding that the world was in imminent danger of coming to a cataclysmic end. For us, some 2,000 years later, the teaching of Paul on social issues has to be revised in the light of historical reality. The world did not come a cataclysmic end!

As a man of his day, Paul wrote about slavery as though it were an irrelevance. In 1 Corinthians 21-24, Paul implies that being in the condition of a slave should not be a matter of concern to the Christian. Sadly, this passage was quoted gleefully by the slave traders as evidence for biblical support of their vile activities. For Paul, the condition of being a slave was an unknown experience. He was part of an educated elite, and he was a citizen of the Roman Empire, which gave him civil rights which were denied to most other people in occupied Judaea. He could never have imagined the rise of the idea of personal freedom from slavery as a major political issue, after centuries of the masses accepting their abject state as 'God-given'.

Fundamentalist Christians are therefore obliged not only to oppose the Council's policy of equal opportunities for gays and lesbians, women and girls, but also for black people. It is by no means an accident that one of the major supports for Apartheid in South Africa came from Christians who found in the Bible justification for their subjugation of non-white people, and their refusal to accept blacks as having any rights to citizenship on equal terms with the ruling whites.

Those politicians who wish to ride the fundamentalist bandwagon when it comes to homosexuality will have to jump off it pretty quickly if they wish to avoid also giving support to those who would deny equality to women and blacks, using the same biblical criteria.

But the problems will not end there. If we are to go along with this narrow-minded and pre-scientific view of the Bible, human beings and the natural world, we will have to start condemning many other things as well. And we will have to forget such 'incidentals' as compassion and understanding, forgiveness and renewal. We will, for example, have to condemn divorce and abolish it completely. Those who divorce will be labelled 'sinners'. Those who commit adultery will be executed, as in Leviticus 20:10. This approach will lead all of us into quite a lot of serious problems. Under the fundamentalist reading of the Bible, quite a large number of people stand condemned.

By virtue of their strange and arbitrary views, our fundamentalists reveal that they are unwilling to read the Bible with intelligence, and to take into account the continuing growth of human knowledge." — **Rev Neil Richardson**.

Bishop John Spong of Newark, New Jersey has spoken out bravely against his Church's attitudes to its gay members. He has written a book entitled *Rescuing the Bible from Fundamentalism* (Harper, 1991), and has been quoted as saying that he changed his ideas about homosexuality, which had originally taken the traditional, condemnatory, line...

...because a, the scientific data has completely changed our interpretation b, there are many, many more gays around than evangelicals ever admit, and c, it's absurd to accept biblical pronouncements uncritically. For the Church not to support committed relationships has the effect of giving its support for promiscuity. When is the Church going to be honest? We've had gay priests and gay bishops for ever...Most mainline Christians are biblically illiterate. Most think the Bible dropped out of heaven fully written in the King James version. You have to explain that Jesus died according to our best estimates in about 30AD and the first Gospel is not until 65AD at the very earliest, so for 35 years everything we know about Jesus circulated by word of mouth. It then got translated into Greek, which Jesus never spoke. Did he wander round the streets of Jerusalem saying 'Oh, by the way, I'm the living bread, I'm the living water'? I do think he is that — but it's not a direct quotation.

In Britain, the ex-Bishop of Durham, Dr David Jenkins, also hit out at those whom he considers 'morally righteous' in his book *Free to Believe* (BBC Books):

> Homosexuals will always be a minority, but they are not unnatural nor in any moral or human sense abnormal. It is to the shame of the church and society that we have not yet learnt how to respond to this reality with clarity...homosexuals have come to be denounced and pilloried in a manner which amounts to persecution, whatever the newly active morally righteous might say...I see a significant number of godly, caring and gentle persons who happen to be homosexual. I know the ministry of many homosexual priests to have been greatly blessed: I value the friendship of many such men and their caring qualities are obvious to anyone.

The Bishop says that if he is called to take a stand on homosexuality "I hope I have the grace to stand with those persons who are attacked for their homosexuality alone for I am certain that is where Jesus Christ would stand, with persecuted and oppressed human beings."

A more recent development, and a much more morally suspect one, has been the use by some fundamentalist churches of AIDS as "proof" that homosexuality is sinful. It was proposed by some Christians that AIDS was "the wrath of God" on homosexuals for their wickedness. Such a crude argument did not stand up to much examination. The first weakness in it is that AIDS is, on a global scale, overwhelmingly a disease which affects heterosexuals. Seventy per cent of those afflicted with this horrible condition are heterosexual, mainly in the developing world. The second weakness is the fact that although lesbians are homosexual, they are almost totally unaffected by AIDS. It has to be said that many Christians have seen the dreadful suffering of the gay community because of AIDS and have stepped forward to put their faith into practice and to care for those who are otherwise rejected. With admirable fortitude, those Christians who have devoted themselves to the care of people with AIDS have come to reassess their opinions of gay people. Often those who have been most hostile to homosexuals have changed their opinions after spending some time within the gay community, helping to care for those unfortunate to have been struck down by HIV. Here is the testimony of a worker at a Christian hospice dedicated to the care of those affected by AIDS and HIV infection.

> I came to this work as a challenge to my Christian faith. I felt I had become complacent and comfortable in my image of myself as one of the chosen. I realised that Jesus would not have sat back and seen a great catastrophe overtake people – even people he did not approve of. And so although I had towed the church's line on homosexuality and convinced myself that there was no way out of the Bible's pronouncements on the subject, I decided that I would volunteer for work in the field of AIDS. That brought me to this hospice, where I now work full time. It also brought me to question not only my attitude to homosexuals but my attitude to life in general. That may sound very portentous, but when you live with death as a daily fact of life it gives a whole new perspective. And not always a depressing one. When I see the love and courage and sheer determination of the people who come here, and their families and friends, I am ashamed that I once dismissed them all as sinners unworthy of God's love. I am humbled in the presence of what happens within these walls, the sheer power of the love that is generated by the people who come here not only to die with dignity, but to settle much of what has been unsettled in their lives. Although this is a Catholic establishment, there is no overt religious emphasis. If our clients want religious support, we can provide it, but I am sorry to say that most of the people who come here have rejected religion, mainly because religion has rejected them. They have embraced life, and letting go of it is not easy for them, especially as many are young people who have not completed their business here on earth. Not many of them come back to the fold.

As the Christian church in all its aspects struggles with the difficult and complex issue of homosexuality, a whole plethora of books has been published to help it along. If you are still unconvinced that your child's homosexuality can be accommodated into your Christian lifestyle, read some of these books. Get in touch with the Lesbian and Gay Christian Movement, or one of the gay groups representing other religions and denominations. You'll find some of them listed in the back of this book, and others in the listings section of *Gay Times*. Talk about the topic with people who have honestly examined the subject from a Christian perspective. Don't restrict yourself to those whose minds are already made up and who are determined that Old Testament values will continue to be applied literally in today's world.

If you have read this far and are willing to go on exploring, I am sure that deep in your heart you are beginning to question the fearful condemnations that some Christians apply to their gay and lesbian brethren. Can they really be talking about your beloved child in such terms? Surely you know that you have not raised someone who is deserving of such pitiless scorn

One argument put forward, of course, is that it is not the individual homosexual that is being condemned, but the practice of homosexuality. "Love the sinner, but hate the sin" is a frequently heard cry. But the implication of such a philosophy demands from homosexual people something that very few heterosexuals are prepared to give. It demands that homosexuals literally give up sex.

Celibacy is a calling that some people feel, but it is a specialised way of life that demands great self-sacrifice. Not everyone wants such a life, and that applies to gay people, too. To demand that homosexuals should not explore their feelings to the full is selfish and unreasonable. Homosexuals are human beings, and as we've said in previous chapters, they want the same things that everyone else wants: love, and a close companion with whom that love can be shared in all its aspects. This isn't much to ask, surely?

Your child is probably not cut out for a life of denial and celibacy. If this is the case, then surely he or she should be encouraged to live as good and useful a life as possible? The happiness that a full, loving and sexual relationship can bring should be the right of everyone — gay or straight. There need not necessarily be any overwhelming religious objections to two people loving each other.

Other Christian sects would have us believe that homosexuals can be "rescued" from their lifestyle by prayer. Some even say that it is possible to "convert" homosexuals into heterosexuals simply by asking God for such a miracle. They will even produce examples of "ex-gay" people. How can that be explained? Well, it's possible that some people move along the sexual spectrum at different times in their lives. As the sexologist Alfred Kinsey demonstrated, sexual preference is not necessarily a simple choice of gay/straight, but can be layered in degrees. Sometimes people who are basically heterosexual will, at some stage in their life, have a homosexual relationship. This does not mean that they are gay. Similarly, homosexuals who have heterosexual relationships are not necessarily straight. And so people do sometimes appear to change. In fact they haven't changed — they're just expressing a different aspect of the same personality. Your child might well have a heterosexual component in his or her sexual character, but it may only be a small part and they may feel happier and more comfortable defining themselves as gay. Because there is, or has been, a heterosexual component, does not mean that your child will, one day, decide to take up a heterosexual way of life. If they do, then that is a choice that they must make based on what they feel, not on what someone else is demanding of them. We have seen the results of people trying to deny their homosexuality by entering into marriages that were disastrous for all concerned.

Other gay people who are deeply religious feel that they have to place their personal needs after what they see as their duty to God. By sheer effort of will and self-denial they suppress their homosexuality. This does not necessarily make them happy people, but for such individuals, happiness comes a poor second to religious observance. Suppressing such deeply-rooted feelings can be damaging, but it is a choice that some people make. They should not put their own personal decision up as an example to other people. For the vast majority of gay people, such self-denial and repression will seem like a denial of life itself.

It is less than useless insisting that people 'change' their sexual orientation to order – it can't be done. Not even with prayer. To go down this path of enforced denial is to store up a lifetime of misery, repression and ultimate disappointment. By refusing to accept your child's sexuality you will either lose him or her completely, or create ever more barriers between you.

One woman who struggled with the question of Christianity and homosexuality in relation to her gay son, was Mary V. Borhek, who wrote movingly of her slow progress to acceptance in a book called *My Son Eric* (Pilgrim Press, 1979). Only after many years of painful personal exploration did she reach the conclusion that:

If we view the Bible as an iron-bound wooden box, nailed together from stout timbers, which contains God and the rules for the world, we are going to run into no end of difficulties. If we try to attach scientific accuracy to biblical statements that are intended to be symbolic, we find ourselves in another kind of dilemma. If, however, we view the Bible as the record of how people perceived God through long ages, then we are beginning to get on the right track. Certainly the God who is portrayed at some places in the Old Testament is far different from the God who is revealed in Jesus. This does not mean that God has changed through the ages. Only our understanding of God has changed...The day of simplistic answers is over. We cannot rap out a pat rule and feel we have covered the situation...If the Church does say 'Jesus loves gays and lesbians', can its only further message to them be that because they can't live out their sexual lives in the normal ways, they cannot have any sexual lives at all? If the message to heterosexual persons was 'In order to enter the kingdom of God you have to forego all sexual life', I wonder how many heterosexual people would choose to enter the kingdom?

Moving from total inability to accept her son, Mary Borhek eventually arrived at a stage where not only could she accept and embrace him – and his sexuality – but felt that she, too, had grown in stature and compassion. The journey she had undertaken had led her into a new understanding she could not have envisioned at the start. Now she has recognised the pain that her son had endured in the years when he was silent, and she has elected to do whatever she can to help others who are going through the same experience. She has worshipped in a gay church and campaigned for equal rights for homosexuals. She says: "I am going forth to help repair the devastations of many generations. The long dark night of my soul has passed; the days of my mourning have ended. I have stepped forth, at last, into a morning of joy."

You, too, can have your own morning of joy, even though it is preceded by a long dark night of struggling. All it takes, as Mary Borhek found, is a determination to find the right answers, and to keep searching until those answers are found. You will know when you've arrived, because at that stage you will stop worrying and all will become clear.

Another mother who has experienced a similar, long search sums it up as follows:

> It seemed that the more information I found the more confused I became. I prayed and I talked and I read more and more books. I tried to see it from every point of view, and not restrict myself only to a single perspective. It was several years before I suddenly came to the conclusion that I was on the right track. I had read extensively about homosexuality from medical, sociological and religious points of view. All this information had gone into my mind and had a good old swirl around. Somehow the answers came out of it all — answers that were good enough for me. I started to calm down, to dismantle the wall of misunderstanding that stood between my son and myself. Over that period I came to realise that I was losing my fear. I am not saying that it was a divine revelation, but I had certainly asked God to guide me through my researches and to help me sort the wheat from the chaff. I love my son as much as ever, and I find no difficulty in reconciling that love with my love of God.

Other religions are also struggling and having much the same problems as Christianity. Jewish denominations vary in their approaches almost as much as Christian ones do. The more liberal synagogues have little problem integrating their gay members, whilst more orthodox congregations are still hostile and condemning. Many of the things that have been written about Christian approaches will apply here, but there are other problems which are unique to Jewish culture. I suggest that any parent from a Jewish community who wants to hear the other side of the argument should contact the Jewish Lesbian and Gay Helpline (see listings at the back of this book), for more information. If that seems too difficult at the moment, a chat with a sympathetic rabbi might be helpful – one who is well-informed on the issue and who won't just intone traditional orthodoxy.

Ethnic Communities

Gay people who live in minority ethnic communities have special problems. They face possible discrimination on many levels: they may, for instance, encounter racism both in mainstream society and in the gay community, and they may face homophobia in their ethnic community as well as in the wider culture in which they are living.

In most ethnic minority communities the family is the moving force. It becomes a bulwark against the hostility of the majority culture, and it is an important resource and support for all its members. Gay people within those families must think long and hard before they come out, because if their family takes the news badly and rejects them, the consequences could be disastrous. When a gay person becomes an outcast from his or her ethnic community there is an intense and unique sense of isolation; the essential supports against racism are removed. The rejected person can feel as though he or she has been uprooted and left without an identity. Such people – who often feel like outcasts from their own culture as well as the majority culture – may occasionally drift into antisocial and destructive activities such as drug-taking, crime and prostitution.

Even those who have been materially successful and are lucky enough to be able to disregard the financial disadvantages that often go with minority ethnic status, can feel a profound sense of isolation. This was illustrated by the black soccer player Justin Fashanu, who made a public coming out via the pages of the tabloid press. The black community in Britain immediately reacted with hostility. *The Voice*, a newspaper for the black community, wrote in critical terms of the athlete's decision to tell the world he was gay. It quoted a spokesman from the Nigerian High Commission in London explaining that until recently homosexuality was punishable by death there. "In Nigeria we treat homosexuals with utter contempt. Homosexuality is still illegal in Nigeria...I can assure you that the Nigerian people as a whole do not like them." Justin's brother, John (also a famous soccer player), was quoted as saying that Justin was "an outcast" and vowing never to speak to him again because of the "shame" he had brought on the family.

The Voice also reported the reaction of its readers to the story:

The Voice's report on soccer star Justin Fashanu's gay 'coming out' has provoked a mixed response from readers. Many phoned our offices to complain about anti-gay attitudes in the black community, saying our story did not help their cause. At the same time others phoned us stating strong anti-gay sentiments. They felt we should not be covering stories about gays. Andrew Watson from Birmingham echoed the attitude of many young men who phoned us. 'Justin Fashanu ain't no black man. People like him just bring shame on us. We have enough negative images without more being added. I don't want white people saying black men are batty men [a contemptuous West Indian term for homosexuals].

It took a long campaign by black gay pressure groups to get *The Voice* to put the other side of the story. The paper eventually carried an interview with Justin. It was obvious that the thing that had hurt him most was the rejection he had suffered from most of his family (his sister had stuck by him and offered him a home until he sorted himself out). Justin is quoted as saying: "Those who say you can't be black and gay and proud of it are simply ignorant. I have no time for it."

Two such people seem to be his own brothers. John's attacks on him in the press and cool response to Justin's wish to return to league football have pained him deeply. "It's a heartache when you have a reaction like that from a brother you love. It would be easy for me to be unforgiving to my brothers John and Philip, but I love them".

The Fashanu affair at least gave the black community food for thought. Although there was much intolerance and aggression, there were also signs that a well of understanding exists. Justin Fashanu has been unlucky in having a family that, in the main, rejects him because of his sexuality. It is obvious from what he has said in public that it is this aspect of the whole affair that has hurt him most. So, why did he do it? *The Voice* interviewer says: "He wants to be a new type of role-model, to prevent cases like that of a gay young man he met while playing football in Canada who was so unhappy about his family's rejection of him that he committed suicide." Surely Justin Fashanu should be admired for his courage, generosity of spirit and selflessness not persecuted and made into a pariah.

Eventually *The Voice* made the connection between racism and homophobia and in another editorial said:

Black people know only too well what it's like being treated as second class citizens. Unfortunately the experience of racism has not given us as greater degree of tolerance or understanding when it comes to accepting those who are different to ourselves. The treatment of gays and lesbians in our community is proof of this. The black community is generally hostile and damning of its gay brothers and sisters, displaying the sort of narrow-minded ignorance we normally associate with bigots and racists. Can we morally demand equality and respect, if we are denying the same to members of our own community?

Perhaps the most telling sentence of all from *The Voice*'s many reports on Justin Fashanu said: "Cut off from his family, he describes his last six months as the loneliest time of his life."

Survival In A Hostile Community

Surveys among lesbians and gay men from Asian communities have uncovered a survival mechanism which is quite commonly used; it has been called "covering." The lesbian or gay man aims for some great academic, financial or entrepreneurial achievement which is valued by the family above social interaction. The family will be satisfied by this great success and the gay person will be excused from following the traditional route of marriage and children. After all, he or she will have much more important things to do! This does not mean that such a person will necessarily express themselves homosexually. If they did so they would risk losing their hard-earned prestige and might find much hostility from their family. But such a strategy will at least relieve them of engaging in heterosexual relationships which they don't want.

If you live within an ethnic community and you suspect your child is gay – or if he or she has already told you – then there are added considerations you need to take into account. There is a special obligation upon you, which does not apply so strongly to parents from the white majority.

1. Your support is an essential prerequisite to your child getting through life successfully in a culture that is fundamentally racist. If you withdraw that support and react in a hostile and rejecting manner, it is possible that you will cause long-lasting damage to your son or daughter. In a society that discriminates against your child because of his or her colour as well as their sexuality, he or she needs the unique support that your family can give. Unlike in the white community, there is less opportunity for your child to strike out successfully on his or her own. You don't need to be told that people from ethnic minorities have special problems finding work, accommodation and friends in the dominant white society; your child has the extra pressure of being gay, which also might work against him or her in the world at large. The powerful nurturing aspects of your family should not be denied to your gay daughter or son.

2. If you deny your child unqualified support in their chosen lifestyle, you may be alienating him or her from their roots, their culture, their language, their food and their religion. Although your child may appear to downplay and devalue these things, they are nevertheless important elements for a balanced life even for the most westernised of young people.

3. Your community may be hostile to the idea of having open lesbians and gay men living within it. If this is the case, then you may want to keep the news of your child's sexual orientation within the family. It is up to you to judge who you can safely tell and who you cannot.

4. Most young people from minority ethnic cultures have problems adapting. For the lesbian and gay person this is made even more difficult for the reasons we've already stated. Your child may be displaying signs of disturbance because of the intense and varied pressures on him or her. If you see signs of psychological illness — depression, aggression or even suicidal tendencies — you may be able to find support from your doctor. But remember what has been written already in this book: not all doctors are well-informed, and if your child is suffering because of his or her sexuality, ensure that it is not made worse by an ignorant GP or priest.

In Hindu, Sikh and Islamic communities, religion and culture are more closely linked than they are elsewhere in Britain. Most of what is referred to as the "Christian community" is, in fact, secular in its cultural life. Only a very small proportion of the mainstream population go to church or express their religious convictions in a formal way. For ethnic minorities, however, it is, in the main, different. Religion pervades many aspects of day to day living, and there seems to be little room for homosexuality in communities which are so heavily family-centred.

Some efforts are being made to change attitudes within the Hindu and Islamic communities, but these are tentative at present and have made little impact. It is difficult to know how parents from these communities react to their child's homosexuality should it ever come to their attention and perhaps this is an area that is ripe for exploration. However, if you are the parent of a gay child from such a community, and you have a traditional outlook on life, all I can suggest is that you examine your heart, read the rest of what is contained in this book, and try to make sense of it in your own way. The reactions of your family and neighbours will probably not fit the pattern of those who have been interviewed for this book and, if you decide to be honest with them, you can probably expect a deal more hostility and rejection than your white counterparts.

It may be helpful to know, though, that other people from your community have coped with this problem before you, and many more will do so in the future. They have recognised the special problems faced by their gay son or daughter and have made special efforts to come to terms some of them very successfully.

If you want to help your child to adjust to being gay, and to support him or her through the troubled times, then you might encourage them to join a lesbian and gay group created within their own culture. There are several black groups in operation as well as Asian-oriented groups. Within such groups your child can find the support and understanding that is needed to help them make the adjustment to life as a black gay man or lesbian.

9.
Regaining happiness

Is it possible ever to get over the shock of discovering your child is gay? Will you ever be able to embrace him or her wholeheartedly again and really accept their sexuality?

Some readers will already be saying a resounding, positive "yes"; some will still have reservations but will be feeling less anxious than they did at the beginning. Yet others will remain dreadfully upset and will be answering, "no, no, a thousand times no!"

If you've come this far and still haven't been convinced that you can change the negative to the positive, then let's look a little more closely at the things that may be standing in your way.

Why is it that some people can accept so easily, whilst others struggle mightily with their conscience? Research has shown that there are two types of people who are least likely to be able to come to terms with their homosexual child. The first is the deeply religious person who is sincerely convinced that homosexuality can never be sanctioned because of biblical teaching. To such people, the chapter on religion earlier in this volume will have remained unconvincing. They will be unable to see the logic of these alternative ways of interpreting the Bible and will cling to the traditional, literal teachings. They see no way out of their dilemma.

Secondly, conservative individuals who have a high regard for convention and the status quo may also be resisting the acceptance of their child's homosexuality. For them, society's rules and regulations are paramount. They are not comfortable with individuals who, by choice or circumstance, live outside the strict parameters set by our culture. Homosexuality is one of the stronger taboos and, for the ultra conventional, quite beyond the pale.

Both types of people – the conventional and the religious – feel safest if there is a "proper" way to do things, if there are dependable rules by which to live. They respect authority and do their best to live by the letter of the law even if that law is, at times, an ass. There is little room in the lives of the conventional for anything which transgresses the supposed norm. Indeed, many of the ideas in this book will have seemed subversive to such people, they will have tutted, shuddered and maybe even thrown the whole thing into the bin. As with most areas of life, the conventionally minded individual person will not see sexual activity as being open to much interpretation: there is a "norm" and anything which deviates from it is "wrong", "bad", "immoral", "unnatural" or just plain incomprehensible. Such conservative people aren't happy with grey areas. Any ambiguity in sexual matters is most disturbing to them.

The conventionally-minded person will be fazed by feminism and puzzled by gay rights. How could anyone want to buck the rules like this? Surely everyone knows that sex should be between men and women for the purpose of procreation? The idea of "recreational" sex – even between men and women – is often distasteful to such people.

And what happens to gay people who are raised with such rigid values and have internalised them to the extent that they become fixed? The sad fact is that often they will turn the hatred they have been taught for homosexuality back in on themselves. They will probably live lives of enormous propriety, probably marrying in order to keep up appearances. They will become exceedingly intolerant of anything which contradicts the status quo. They are, in effect, running away from the truth about themselves. This phenomenon has been called "the breast plate of righteousness" by the American sociologist Laud Humphreys. He observed it in men who were leading a secret homosexual life, while at the same time appearing to be pillars of the establishment. Sometimes these men went so far as to become "moral crusaders", demanding that homosexuals should be persecuted and discriminated against. This helped reinforce in their own minds — and in the minds of those around them – that they were "normal".

A third sort of person who could be having difficulty coping with their gay child is the "macho man". Many heterosexual men feel that homosexuality presents some kind of threat to their own sexuality. They are often insecure and lack real self-esteem. These are the men who, when they're with a group of friends, like to demonstrate how truly manly they are by making crude sexist and homophobic remarks. They will often depend on alcohol to give them the courage to do the things they want to do. This sometimes leads to very anti-social behaviour, demonstrating their contempt for women and hatred of gay men through wife-beating and gay-bashing.

This intolerance and inability to accept other people who are different is what happens when the mind falls into the convention trap. Unable to shake off the black-and-white approach to life, there comes a point when there is only one answer to every question – which is either yes or no, or right or wrong.

Do you recognise some aspects of yourself here? Please understand, I am not making any blanket condemnation of people who respect traditional values or rules. Indeed, if we didn't have rules, society would soon be insufferably chaotic. In many ways, people who exercise self-control and respect for institutions are the backbone of the country: duty, community values, the respect of neighbours and friends are worthwhile, but there can be qualifications: values may need reconsidering when they are so rigid that they actually destroy the quality of life. After all, the breakdown of the family is a pretty traumatic event for anyone — for people who look upon the family as the basic building block of society, it might seem like the end of the world. Even so, rigidity of thinking prevents the ultra-conventional from seeing beyond the unfairness and injustice that is being aimed at their homosexual child. The need to uphold society's rules and regulations overwhelms even parental love and the instinct to protect.

The people whose lives are ruled by "shoulds" and "musts" and "oughts" are the people who will be having most problems with the knowledge of their son's or daughter's sexuality. If you often find yourself saying that people "should" do this, or "ought" to do that, then you might be storing up disillusion for yourself. Trying to control other people – even those for whom you feel a particular responsibility – will lead to constant conflict and resistance. For evidence of this, you only need look at the number of people who are raised and educated in religious institutions and then go on to become rebels of the first order. Convent girls are notorious rule-breakers and so are those men educated by monks. The more severe the upbringing, it seems, and the greater the urge to resist it in later life.

You may feel that you've raised your children to behave well in society. You have told them that they "should" obey the rules (even when those rules are patently foolish); you've told them they "ought" to behave themselves at all times (although it robs them of any spontaneity); and you've shown by example that authority "must" be respected, even if it is unjust.

However, your child's sexuality is not a rebellion against his or her upbringing. That upbringing, though, might well be the cause of much misery in their life. Just as your own strict and rigid childhood caused you to fear anything that contradicted the conventions of society, so your child will be struggling to reconcile his or her nature with what they've been taught to believe is the "proper" way to live. So, for their sake, perhaps the time has come to make a small deviation from the path of certainty. Society must develop and evolve with changing circumstances. This does not mean, of course, that you have to take on board every fad and fancy that comes along. In homosexuality we are not talking about a fashion that will pass, like mini-skirts, we are talking about an aspect of human nature which has been around since anyone can remember. It should be a cause for celebration, not misery, that society has reached the point where it does not need to persecute homosexuals quite so ferociously as it has done in the past. We are becoming more civilised and compassionate. Surely this must be an advance.

Thinking for yourself and challenging the received wisdom is unsettling, but when your family is at stake there can be no room for complacency. If you persist in your efforts to change, you'll also find it exhilarating. Taking this untrodden road will teach you much about your child and yourself.

If you make the effort you will not have to inflict the kind of cruelty upon your son or daughter that I have seen other parents inflict. Some have gone so far as to turn their youngsters away from the home they treasured – all because parents were unable to bear the 'shame' of their child's sexuality. Those parents placed more emphasis on what other people thought than on the needs of their own offspring.

As you've read through this book, you have seen that there is a substantial body of scientific and sociological evidence indicating that homosexuality is not "chosen", nor is it changeable at will. If you cannot accept this evidence on face value, then all you have to do is to peep over the barrier that you've erected between yourself and your child and have a look for yourself. Become your own sociological researcher and make a first hand study of your son's or daughter's life and that of his or her friends. You'll be able to make your own mind up then whether your conviction that it is "wrong" is justified or not.

But even taking a non-committal look means that you have to overcome some hurdles. You may still feel quite strongly that all your prejudices about homosexuals will be confirmed, so what's the point of even challenging them? If they are confirmed, you've lost nothing, but if they aren't, then you've got your child back and a new knowledge about one important aspect of their life. All that you have to do is give it a little time. Continue to be wary if you must, but at least listen to the other side of the story.

Maybe this book has shown you that there are other ways of looking at homosexuality which you perhaps hadn't thought of. After all, you've heard enough of the bad stuff, it's time you balanced it out with some of the good. You have something to gain from finding out what is really true and what is myth and legend, handed down unquestioned over the centuries. You have a great deal to lose if you don't make any effort at all.

"But," say some parents, "this is a challenge to the very core of my religious belief. If I change my stance on this, then the Bible becomes meaningless."

I would refer those parents back to what was written in the chapter on religion. Some of the laws written in Leviticus are, by today's standards, completely unacceptable and impractical, not to mention barbaric. The fact that you choose to observe some of these laws and disregard others is the key. Stephen Fry put this very succinctly in an article in *The Daily Telegraph* (12 July 1991):

There are a couple of passages from Leviticus where it is explicitly stated that it is 'an abomination' for a man to lie with another as with a woman. These are eagerly seized upon by those who would wish to demonstrate the wickedness of homosexuality. Neighbouring passages which state, with equal fervour, that thou shalt not wear a garment made from two different kinds of stuff, nor round off thine hair at the temples, nor mar the edges of thy beard, nor make any tattoos upon thyself, nor breed one kind of cattle with another, these are cheerfully ignored. Yet Leviticus states that all statutes must be obeyed, from kosher food to the sacrifices of a lamb (or two turtle doves if you cannot afford a lamb) made by a woman who has purified herself after giving birth. In the case of bearing a male child, of course, a mother is unclean for seven days; if the baby is female she is defiled for two whole weeks. One is not given the option of picking and choosing between these eccentric commands.

If we tried unquestioningly to apply the whole of Leviticus to the twentieth century, we would end up with a very cruel and callous society. Those laws were formulated for a time and place that bears little similarity to our world today. What modern science has discovered about homosexuality was not known to the lawmakers of old. Just as modern animal husbandry and hygiene has eliminated the need for some of the Biblical restrictions on food, so our understanding of human nature has made us realise that much of what Leviticus demands is cruel. Can you imagine stoning adulterers to death? Or forbidding women to teach? Or banning the eating of shellfish?

The fact that some religious leaders continue to insist that the biblical laws relating to homosexuality should remain intact (whilst other restrictions, relating to different matters, can be conveniently ignored), doesn't mean that those leaders are right. Gradually, and with much resistance, opinions are changing. Although some traditionalist Christians are advocating harder attitudes towards gay people, many others are coming to the conclusion that homosexuals are just like everyone else except in one small way. Many religious people have accepted the scientific findings about homosexuality and have modified their approach accordingly. There is no shame in this, no defeat. As Methodist Minister, Leonard Barnett wrote, in his book *Homosexuality, Time To Tell The Truth* (Gollancz, 1975):

People will still sometimes confuse gayness and gay behaviour; the fact of homosexuality in human life, with its outward expression. They identify, wrongly, being and doing. We might well say 'Is sex wrong?' as to say, 'Is homosexuality wrong?' Forgive this elementary point. But one still hears people asking just that question – or asserting that homosexuality is wrong – without being aware that they are talking nonsense. One might as well ask if money, or ambition, or power is wrong. The answer is the same to all such questions. It begins with the old phrase, 'It all depends...' The thing itself – money, power, sex homosexuality, or whatever – is neither right or wrong, in the setting of actual people making actual decisions and acting in one way or another.

If religious conflict is the source of your inability to accept, then continue to struggle. Read and talk widely, don't just take one opinion and accept it as the final word. Maybe one day, you'll be able to see that by adjusting some of your beliefs in the light of modern knowledge, you do not have to undermine the whole of your faith.

Don't worry if you can't manage it instantly, these big life events take time. Be kind to yourself and recognise that it's usual and understandable to have an occasional flash of doubt – or even a full-scale crisis of conscience – along the way. Parents often report the see-saw effect of their adjustment. This is how Dilys reported it:

One day I'd be happy, and imagining that everything was going to be OK. I'd got myself over the shock, and was coming to terms with Edward's way of life. Then suddenly I'd plunge into this deep depression, and all the old worries would come back. He was going to die from AIDS, I thought, or he's going to be miserable all his life, with everyone hating him. And then he'd come over to see me, and I'd see his smiling face and realise that he wasn't maladjusted at all, he was having a great life. And I'd relax again. I kept going up and down like this for ages – years, in fact. But that seems to have passed. I'm much more relaxed about the whole thing. Edward is very successful in his job, and has a very pleasant friend. In many ways he's a privileged young man. All right, so he isn't going to do what I expected with his life, but now I've adjusted to that, the alternative he's chosen isn't so bad. I've managed to throw out all the worries I had about him. We're far closer now than we have been before, and I realise this is because he no longer has to pretend that he's someone he isn't. How can you have an honest relationship with anyone if you're telling lies all the time? Now he trusts me with his worries, and I feel honoured about that."

If their daughter is lesbian, parents may have problems not only coping with her homosexuality, but also with the fact that she is a strong, independent women. "Women aren't supposed to be so pushy," is a frequent cry from some parents, alarmed to see their daughters as resourceful, self-reliant individuals who don't need men to support them. Fathers especially seem alarmed by this strength and feel it "isn't right" in a way that they can't quite explain. They will tell you that they believe in the equality of women and that everyone should have the same opportunities, but at the same time they will be uneasy when they see such a philosophy in action. Whereas they might be proud of their son's achievements, they are slightly bemused by their daughter's success. Once again, this might be the product of a conventional upbringing, and it's necessary to issue a very basic challenge to the received wisdom.

It seems that mothers are likely to be more understanding of their child's sexuality than fathers. Fathers frequently feel threatened by male homosexuality and disturbed by the thought of sexually aggressive women – which is how they perceive lesbians. The fact that their daughter might take a sexual initiative and play a dominant role with another woman is almost impossible for some fathers to comprehend.

All these barriers need to be faced and challenged. It can be done, and here are some of the people who have succeeded.

Wilhelmina is a fifty-three year old woman of West Indian descent. She lives in west London with her husband Leroy and their eight children. Her youngest son, Marlon is twenty and gay. Two years ago, he told his mother about his sexual orientation. She was furious, and ordered him out of the house:

> About five minutes after telling Marlon to go, I changed my mind. I've always had a soft spot for him, being the baby of the family, I know you aren't supposed to have favourites, but Marlon's always been special to me. I made him unpack his suitcase. How can you throw your own child on to the street – even if he is a homosexual? He was still Marlon, come hell or high water.
>
> The big problem was with my Baptist church. I love my church and all my friends who go there, and I love the pastor, such a good man. I was so confused that I decided to

go and have a word with him. He was not pleased with what I had to tell him, and he was furious with Marlon for having chosen what he called a 'wicked way of life.' He said that if I brought the boy in to the church, he would pray for Marlon to be delivered from the devil's temptation. The pastor was so angry, I've never seen him like that.

Well, I went home and told Marlon what had happened, and asked what he thought of the idea. He told me that there was no way that he was going to the church, as he didn't have any truck with the devil, so there was nothing to be delivered from. He said the pastor was ignorant and had it all wrong.

In the meantime, he'd told all his brothers and sisters about being a homosexual, and they were all on his side. They told me I was being foolish talking about devils. They're all good kids, so I had to listen to them. I was a bunch of confusion, I can tell you.

My husband Leroy had to know what was happening, and when I told him, he wasn't pleased at all. He said homosexuals were dirty creatures who shouldn't be allowed to share the same space with decent people. I said to him, 'Don't you realise you're talking about your son, our own Marlon?' He was a bit shame-faced, but he still said he couldn't accept any of that stuff, and he didn't want to hear any more about it.

I didn't know what to do. The kids were telling me on the one hand that I was being hysterical and that they were standing firm with Marlon, while my pastor and my husband were telling me that I was harbouring a devil in the family. In the middle of all this was my lovely Marlon. I just couldn't believe he was evil. My mind was telling me that I couldn't have produced anything evil. I've always been good and I've raised my kinds to be good.

I didn't deal with it very well, I just let things drift. I was scared what the congregation was going to say to me if the pastor decided to tell them. Thankfully hc kept it to himself. He occasionally asked me how I was doing, and I'd say things were going along fine. I didn't want to say any more about Marlon, because I didn't want to have another lecture about him being evil.

Eventually I went to the library and got a few books out about the subject of homosexuality. I read some Christian thoughts on the subject, and a lot of them weren't anything to do with what the pastor said and I found that very helpful. I still don't think Marlon is a devil – you couldn't wish to meet a sweeter child, he wouldn't harm a fly and he works voluntarily with handicapped people.

I've now reached the point where it never occurs to me to try to interfere with Marlon's life. He has a right to live in the way that God has ordained for him. Yes, I've come to the conclusion that God has given Marlon his gayness just as he gave me my straightness. I don't know the reason why but, then again, there are a lot of other things I don't know the reason why. God moves in mysterious ways His wonders to perform.

I hope that Marlon will be happy. He seems to be OK at the moment, although sometimes a little lonely. He's not a great mixer, even though I encourage him to go out and about and meet people. There don't seem to be many other gay people in our community – nobody likes 'batty boys' as they're called.

Whatever happens, he knows he's got a home here. The world can be cruel enough to black children without their parents making things worse for them. I'm pleased to say that Marlon has the love and support of his brothers and sisters. They rib him about it sometimes, but they'd stand with him if it came to the crunch. I'm still working on his father, who has this macho thing that won't let him back down. I think he imagines that he'll be thought of as less of a man if his friends and cronies find out about Marlon. It's sad – sadder than Marlon's problems."

Barry is a middle-aged father of three. His daughter Lorraine is a successful businesswoman living in a neighbouring city. It became apparent to Barry that she was living an unconventional life when, one day, he and his wife Teresa went to visit their daughter, and found that another woman, Kay, had moved in.

Teresa was surprised to see this other woman, but she was polite and pleasant to her. Lorraine just introduced us and didn't offer an explanation about who Kay was or on what basis she was living in her house. I suppose she expected us to pick up the message. They've been living together now for about five years, and it seems like it might be a permanent arrangement. We've come to like Kay – she's the absolute opposite of Lorraine, very feminine and petite. Lorraine has always been very bossy and thrusting, which is why, I suppose, she's so successful with her business. Kay seems to have softened her a bit. Lorraine relaxes better when she's at home. She doesn't depend so much on work for the focus of her life. I think it's a good thing to have a balance. In a way we didn't have a lot of problem because we never thought about them as being lesbians, just as being Lorraine and Kay, our daughter and her friend.

It's sometimes difficult to know how to include them in family celebrations. Most people just accept them at face value and don't ask about their relationships – not directly, any way. What they say behind our backs is a different matter. But I don't think there is a great deal of hostility, everyone is very positive towards them. Neither Lorraine nor Kay make much fuss about the family, anyway. They make an effort to keep up contact with me, but they don't bother much with the others. They have their own life, and that's up to them. I have grandchildren from my other children, so that's not too much of a disappointment. I just treat everyone as an individual.

Parents' Groups

As the numbers of homosexuals who have decided to come out increases, so more and more parents are faced with the dilemma of having a gay son or daughter. Many of these mothers and fathers feel isolated with what they imagine is a rare and insoluble problem. They need to talk to others who had already successfully survived the trauma.

Those who have navigated the choppy waters of adjustment have recognised this ongoing need for support and information. and have formed voluntary helping agencies.

One of the first, and most famous, was Parents' Enquiry, founded many years ago by the indefatigable Rose Robertson. Mrs Robertson had two sons – one gay and one straight. In an interview she has told about the anger she felt when she first found out about her son and how, eventually, she turned it away from her son and on to the external forces that were persecuting him. As a trained social worker she recognised the need for a support service for the thousands of parents who were "going through hell." With enormous energy she established a pattern of professionalism which has been much copied throughout the world. Rose Robertson has also been a tireless campaigner for the rights of homosexuals, and has spoken out for law reform and social acceptance.

Parents' Enquiry is now known throughout the United Kingdom, and has helped hundreds of families through their crises. Others, inspired by Rose Robertson's commitment have followed her example. Some of the newer groups provide a telephone helpline, others have personal contact and group meetings.

Even though there are more groups around than there used to be, there still aren't enough to cover the whole country. Therefore, you may have to make a few long-distance calls or travel a little further in order to take advantage of their services. It will be worth it. It cannot be emphasised enough just how important it is for you to talk over your feelings with someone who has already been there and survived. For some people a chat with a successful role model is often all that is needed. The reassurance offered by parents who have accepted their gay child and lived to tell the tale is immeasurably valuable.

If you are experiencing problems which seem, at the time, unbearable – and it is the lucky few who don't – then please contact one of these agencies. You'll find a list in the back of this book. Naturally this list could become out of date quite quickly as many of the groups are voluntary and depend very much on the commitment of workers and the availability of funds. With that in mind I would suggest that if you find that any particular group has ceased to operate that you buy a current issue of *Gay Times* for the latest listing. You could also think of ringing Lesbian and Gay Switchboard, which is also listed at the back of the book. They have the latest information.

Parents' support groups are a valuable resource in your journey to acceptance and you should make full use of them. Listen to Helen, who contacted just such a group a couple of years ago when she was "totally shattered" by her son's coming out:

I went to the library and somehow managed to unearth this telephone number of a local helpline for the parents' of gays. I rang them with great apprehension. I had absolutely no idea what to expect, and was ready to ring off if they said anything that I didn't like. I hadn't told anyone about David's news and I was bursting to talk to someone. I couldn't tell anyone I knew, though, I was so ashamed I don't think I could have got the words out.

Anyway, the woman on the parents' helpline couldn't have been nicer. She understood precisely what I was saying – her own son was gay, and she told me that she had felt exactly the same way as I did when she'd first found out. She told me to take my time and not do anything I would regret. I can't tell you what a relief it was to be able to talk to this woman. She told me a little bit about her own son, and how she had now come to terms with it completely. She said I could ring her any time I wanted. And believe me, I did ring her – every night for a week. She was so patient and she let me talk and talk, and she told me all the things I wanted to hear. She didn't think I was being selfish or silly, but she did say that I was making progress. It didn't seem like it to me, but after a while I started to realise that I was less worried about it. I was sleeping at night again, and even managed to ask David a few questions. At the beginning I hadn't even been able to mention it, I just left the room if he tried to talk. Now we're getting on much better.

Other parents have made such progress that they not only fully accept their son or daughter, they actually feel strongly enough to fight to make life better for them. This they do in many ways, by political campaigning, writing occasional letters to newspapers, contributing money to sympathetic pressure groups, giving talks to other groups that are interested.

Leslie and Jack have a lesbian daughter, Marian. Here is how they feel about the present situation:

Jack and I were accepting of our daughter, and we imagined that she would just be able to quietly get on with her life. Then we heard some of the things that politicians were saying about lesbians and gays, and we started getting angry. It seemed to us that some of these politicians had absolutely no regard at all for the consequences of what they were saying. It was at the time of the Section 28 debate in Parliament. We followed that quite closely because Marian was making such a song and dance about it at home. She was telling us that it was the most serious threat to her civil rights for many years. We thought she was exaggerating, until we started hearing these MPs on the radio, saying the most terrible things about lesbians and gays – things we knew weren't true. And then we read the parliamentary report of the debate over this clause in the Local Government Bill. We were horrified at what was said by people who ought to know better. We found it hard to credit that people could be so ignorant and bigoted.

We knew at that point that we couldn't just sit by and watch this happen – we had to do something about it. So we went on a demonstration in London and marched with other parents of gays. We met some nice people, and felt very good about having done our bit. We wrote a letter to our local paper after our MP said he supported the Clause, and we wrote one to him telling him that he wouldn't be having our vote in future, and we'd encourage other people not to vote for him, too. The letter in the paper had our name attached to it, which was quite a step to take. A few people congratulated us on it, and we felt we'd come out good and proper. All our neighbours knew we had a gay daughter, and just for a change we didn't really care what they thought about it. This was a matter of principle that we thought was more important than the opinions of the neighbours. As it turned out, we got a lot of support.

We are proud of Marian and we are proud of ourselves. We've come a long way since she told us. We've found out as much about ourselves as we have about her. If you'd told me a couple of years ago that I would be politically active, I'd have laughed at you. But both Jack and I have joined the Liberal Democrats and are active members of the local constituency party. We'd never have done this if it hadn't been for Marian raising our awareness of what was happening over Section 28. It made us examine a lot of what we'd taken for granted, and now here we are, thinking of putting up for the local council.

And so it is clear that progress is possible. From complete bewilderment and dismay, it is possible for parents to move on to become supportive and enthusiastic allies in their child's life. The choice is yours, and for some it will be a harder choice than others.

The journey you'll need to undertake is worthwhile on several counts. First, you will save your relationship with your son or daughter. Second, you will find out much about yourself, your attitudes and your strengths and weaknesses. Finally, you will do something to make life easier for gay men and lesbians in general. Society needs to change, and you can be an agent in that change by simply altering the frame of your mind. From rejection you can move to acceptance, from ignorance to knowledge, from hate to love. You will recognise that if you keep your mind and your heart open to new ideas, you will be a richer person. If you continue to work on your feelings, continue to feed your knowledge with the facts, continue to talk to your child and to others who will support you, then by this time next year I can promise that you will feel very much better than you do now. And the year after that you will wonder what the fuss was about in the first place.

Keep a diary – record your feelings as they are now, and in a year's time make a comparison. I can assure you, you'll have a very pleasant surprise. The final word goes to Jenny, whose son is gay.

If I'm ashamed of anything it is the fact that I ever thought that my son was in any way less my son because he was gay. I cringe when I look back at the thoughts that I had at the beginning, and I realise how naive and uninformed I was. And now when I hear people expressing the same kinds of opinions I used to hold, I take great pleasure in putting them right.

A year ago I would have said all this was a pipe dream, but now I feel strong enough to talk to anyone about it. I am happy with my son and his life and friends. If he has a lover and he's had several – I try to be understanding and accommodating. Sometimes I approve of his choice, sometimes I think it's a mistake. But at least we can talk about it like adults rather than as parent and child.

A year ago I would have hit the roof if I had seen my son showing affection to another man in my house, now it's a matter of course. It doesn't shock me any more. I've come to see that he's entitled to show affection in the way that is right for him. For me there are no half measures. If I accept, I accept completely.

Because I love him, I worry about him and his health. I try not to pester him too much about this, because I know that he is well-informed about AIDS. But we have talked about it, and I feel easier in my mind to know that he is mature and sensible on the issue. He wants to live, and he will not do anything that will put his life at risk.

Strange as it may seem, I feel as if I've grown up as much as my son. In many ways my approach to life was childish and selfish. I wanted people to do as I told them, to be what I wanted them to be. Not just my son, but also other people in my life. My husband left me because of the same problem; I couldn't let him be who he was – I was always trying to change him. That experience and my son's coming out have taught me valuable lessons about relating to other people. I now feel much more confident that if I meet someone else, and have another shot at marriage, I'll be much more likely to succeed.

If any other parent is going through the torture that I went through when I first found out my son was gay, I want to tell them that they can win through. But it isn't their child who has to change, it's the parents. If they don't, they'll lose contact with their child, if not physically, then emotionally. If they don't accept, they'll put a distance between them that will ruin everything. It doesn't actually cost very much in the end, and I'm annoyed with myself that it took me so long to find that out.

There will, no doubt, still be areas of conflict between you and your children. This is ever the case. Parents still "want the best" for their children, and this sometimes translates into manipulation and attempts to control every aspect of their life. If you are aware of this tendency to interfere, to make suggestions that are unwelcome or even to try and impose your own values on to your children, even when they aren't shared, then you can do something to control it. Being aware of it is half the battle.

This is not the book to explore the complex issues of parent-child interaction – there are plenty of others available if you want to read more on this topic. One of them is *If You Really Loved Me*.

by Drs Jordan and Margaret Paul (CompCare Publishers, 1987). This makes many suggestions about how you can counteract conflict in your family and gain in its place closeness and understanding between you. As these two psychotherapists say:

> There are smooth times and rough times that come to all of us in infinitely various patterns like ripples in a stream. However, when families learn to interact with loving involvement, open and respecting each other, acting in loving ways to each other, life is satisfying, even peaceful, and often filled with good times and great pleasure

If this sounds too good to be true – or at least something that is beyond your own ability to achieve – remember that there are still choices available to you, still changes that can be made. If your home life is war-like, full of battles and confrontations, then you can do something to change that. You can find out from confronting the truth of your child's homosexuality in a loving way, how these changes are made.

Breaking old patterns of interaction is difficult, but not impossible. It's a long, slow process, but if you are persistent and determined, you'll get there. Read widely, think deeply, analyse and gain knowledge, about yourself as well as about the other people in your family.

I said earlier in this book that when you had gone through the stages of acceptance of your gay child, you would emerge at the other end a bigger, better person. I stick by that prognosis. If you don't fix your ideas in cement, they will evolve, and you will grow closer to the happiness that everyone longs for.

Useful Contacts

Because so many community groups and organisations are precariously funded and depend entirely on the goodwill of volunteers, they sometimes abruptly cease to exist. If you can't get a response from any of the groups listed here, please contact Lesbian and Gay Switchboard in London (0171-837 7324 – 24 hours a day, all year round). Not only can they provide counselling themselves, they also keep the most comprehensive and up-to-date list of groups and helplines available in the United Kingdom.

PARENTS SUPPORT GROUPS

Families & Friends of Lesbians and Gays (FFLAG)
PO Box 153,
Manchester M60 1LP
0161 628 7621 or 748 3452

in **London**:
Phone: Eileen 0171 791 2854

in **Leicester**:
0116 270 8331 (Frances)
0116 235 9774 (Betty)
01509 238883 (Rachel)

Leeds Parents Friend
c/o Voluntary Action Leeds,
Stringer House, 34 Lupton Street,
Hunslett, Leeds LS10 2QW
Tel: 0113-267 4627 (Joy/Alan)
0113 257 7523 (Valerie)
7.30-11pm.

Leicester 0116-255 0667
7.30-10.30pm

Acceptance Kent
(Sheerness)
01796-661463
Tues-Fri 7-9pm

Parents Together
PO Box 464,
London SE25 4AT
Tel: 0181 650 5268 10am-10pm

Parents Enquiry
Nottingham
01623 921 1302 (Nora)

USA
Parents, Families & Friends of Lesbians & Gays (PFLAG)
1012 14th Street N.W.,
Suite 7000,
Washington D. C. 20005
chapters throughout the USA

BOOKSHOPS

Gay's the Word,
66 Marchmont Street,
London WC1N 1AB
0171 278 7654
large lesbian and gay
bookshop with efficient mail
order service

West & Wilde Bookshop,
24a Dundas Street,
Edinburgh,
Scotland EH3 6QQ
mail order available

Out! Bookshop,
4 & 7 Dorset Street,
off Edward Street,
Brighton
01273 623356

**USA & CANDA
Bookshops**

**A Different Light
Bookshop,**
8853 Santa Monica Blvd,
West Hollywood CA90069
USA .

Giovannis Room,
1145 Pine Street,
Philadelphia PA 19107
(215) 923 2960
Mail order available

Glad Day Bookshop,
598a Yonge Street,
Toronto,
Ontario M4Y 1Z3

MAGAZINES

Gay Times,
Ground Floor,
Worldwide House,
116-134 Bayham Street,
London NW1 0BA
0171 482 2576
available in most newsagents
or by subscription. Large
listings section.

The Pink Paper,
72 Holloway Road,
London N7 8NZ
0171 296 6210
weekly free sheet available
from selected venues or on
subscription.

**USA
The Advocate,**
PO Box 541,
Mt Morris,
IL 61054-7848
Bi-weekly national gay
magazine

RELIGIOUS AND RELATED ORGANISATIONS

**Lesbian and Gay Christian
Movement,**
Oxford House,
Derbyshorc Street,
Bethnal Green,
London E2 6HG
0171-739 1249

Quest
Gay Catholic Group,
BM Box 2585,
London WC1N 3XX
Tel: 0171 792 0234
(Fri-Sun 7-10pm)

Jewish Lesbian and Gay Helpline
0171 706 3123
(Mon & Thurs 7-10pm)

Religious Society of Friends (Quakers)
0171 387 3601

Gay and Lesbian Humanist Association (GALHA),
34 Spring Lane,
Kenilworth,
Warwickshire CV8 2HB
Tel: 01926 58450

AIDS INFORMATION AND SUPPORT

National Aids Helpline
Freephone: 0800 567123
10am-10pm

Terrence Higgins Trust
Advice on all aspects of
HIV/AIDS
0171 831 0330 (office hours)

USA
National AIDS Information Hotline
1-800-342-AIDS

Further Reading:

Family Outing
A guide for parents of gays,
lesbians and bisexuals edited
by Joy Dickens
(Published by Peter Owen
ISBN 0-7206 0961-5)
a collection of letters from
the parents of lesbians and
gay men. Received mixed
reviews.

Is the Homosexual my Neighbour?
Letha Scanzoni and Virginia
Ramey Mollenkott
A Christian viewpoint from
two evangelical authors.
(Published by Harper & Row
ISBN 0-06-067076-2)

Different Daughters
edited by L. Rafkin
pieces written by the mothers
of lesbian daughters.
Pulished by Cleis USA
ISBN: 0-939416-13-1

Ask at your bookshop about
the latest titles on this topic.